DIVORCED AFTER 50

DIVORCED AFTER 50

Your 8-Step Guide to Healing and Renewal

NANCY OSIER, M.S.

ISBN: 978-1-7335480-1-4

Editors: Moriah Howell and Pamela Juarez
Cover design: Daliborka Mijailovic
Formatter: Phillip Gessert
Author photo: Courtesy of Deja Webster

DISCLAIMER

Difference Press
Sequim, WA, USA

DEDICATION

THIS BOOK IS dedicated to my big brother. Ralph has always been my champion and hero. He was eight years old when I was born, and he loved me unconditionally right from the start. He was proud of me and I have always been proud of him.

Ralph taught me to take chances and to laugh at life. He taught me to climb trees, skate, do pull-ups and beat boys in arm wrestling. He defended me against bullies and included me when hanging out with his friends, even though I could be a total pest.

I can talk to my brother about anything. I so appreciate his open-mindedness and his entrepreneurial spirit. He is a hard worker and is incredibly knowledgeable in his field. We have both always wanted to write a book. Now that I am a published author, my goal is to help him become one as well. So here's to my brother, my friend, my inspiration. I love you Ralphie!

TABLE OF CONTENTS

FOREWORD

I T WAS 1994, and I arrived home from work to find his voicemail, "I didn't like the job, I'm coming home. I'll be there in two hours." My then husband of 12 years had gone to Alaska to work on a fishing boat. He was supposed to be gone for three months, but he only stayed one week. That was just long enough for my foster son and I to be able to catch our breath. Long enough for us to stop feeling sick every time we heard his car pull up. Long enough for me to realize that I couldn't continue to allow his angry outbursts and physical explosions to terrorize us. But certainly *not* long enough...

Just before he'd left for Alaska, he had put his huge hands on my foster son's neck. He had never hit me, but he raised his fist at me several times, and screamed into my face on a regular basis. He had a terrifying temper. This was the man I had married at age 20 and had stuck with, through thick and thin. The good-looking guy I fell for in high school.

In our first year of marriage, he cheated on me with a girl who had just turned 18. She put sugar in my car's gas tank, tried to run me off the road, and called me at all hours of the night. We went to a pastor for counseling and he told me, "You can either put a ball and chain on his ankle for life, or you can forgive him and move on." I chose to forgive him, but the sting of betrayal continued to burrow into my heart and gnaw at the back of my mind. After he was in the Navy in San Diego for two years, we decided to move back to Washington, so he could return to college. I had hopes that he would get his degree and finally get a real job. That process would take eight years.

I got in my car and drove aimlessly around the dusty little college town where we'd lived since 1988. Tears were streaming down my face, making it difficult to see where I was going. I had just completed my Bachelor's degree that I'd started in 1980. I was working four hours a day in a tiny insurance office. We were constantly scraping by. By then he'd held at least 30 jobs, and there had also been many periods of unemployment.

As I was driving around in a daze, not even realizing where I was, the song by Annie Lennox came on the radio, "Feels just like I'm walking on broken glass..." I felt like I was choking on broken glass! I drove and sobbed. I didn't want to go home. I didn't want to see him. In that moment, I came to a clear realization. I knew in every fiber of my being that I could no longer stay in the marriage. I had no money and no idea what to do or how to do it, but I had to stop the madness. This was not the life I wanted, for my son or for me.

My son had grown up in various foster homes and he'd been adopted by a couple who beat him black and blue at the age of eight. After Child Protective Services got involved, they decided to return custody back to the state. He had lived with them since he was four. As a baby, Bobby had been thrown and shaken by his birth father. At every turn, he had been abused and rejected. He had moved in with us at age 12. He was a very challenging and angry child. It certainly didn't help that my husband was irritable and explosive. He would corner Bobby with his fist in his face. There was no way I was going to allow this child to be threatened! I had been rendered infertile after my husband cheated on me, and all I'd ever wanted was to be a mother. I loved Bobby like he was my own from the moment he moved in with us.

I had been trying to figure out how I would make it on my own but I hadn't filed for divorce yet, when my husband decided to take a job in a nearby town. He rented an apartment so he wouldn't have to commute. He quickly began charging large amounts of money to furnish his apartment. He even put my car up as collateral on a high interest loan. This seemed like the perfect time to make my move, so I found an inexpensive divorce service and filed papers. I changed the locks on my doors and had him served. I decided to forge ahead on my own by applying to graduate school to become a counselor. We had very little money, so Bobby and I played video games together, played ping-pong at the university, and went fishing at the local pond. Whenever we got stressed, we would escape our little apartment by going for a drive and singing along with the radio. At that time, a popular song was "Life is a Highway" by Tom Cochran. That became our motto when life became challenging. I'd say to him, "Hey, life is a highway." That most always made him laugh and lightened the mood.

I had left the marriage to protect Bobby from being threatened and verbally abused. Although his safety was foremost in my mind, the need to protect him had given me the strength and resolve I needed to also protect myself and create a better future for both of us.

It wasn't easy raising a teenage boy on my own. Once I had the papers served, my ex never saw Bobby again. I had no parenting back-up and no respite. We worked through things, but Bobby tested me even more once I became a single parent. I was working part time, attending graduate school, and working hard to make sure he was busy and supervised.

When we divorced, Bobby was going on 15. I made my home, our little townhouse apartment, a safe haven for him and his friends to hang out in. I let them play video games, took them to the local pond to fish, and to the university to hang out in the games room. But when he turned 16, things started to slip. He started sneaking around and drinking. I regularly checked with his friend's parents, so we all knew what the kids were doing and where they were. I also stayed in frequent contact with his teachers.

Despite all my efforts, he snuck out one night while I was sleeping. He took my car and slid on some ice, wrecking my only mode of transportation. Fortunately, he was not hurt. When I went to get in my car to go to grad school, I discovered a large swath of paint missing on the driver's side. Then I noticed that the side mirror was in the front seat. The steering wheel was also upside-down, because the driveline had broken. It's a miracle he had been able to drive it home safely! Bobby had already gone to school on the bus when I discovered the damage.

Bobby had a difficult past in foster care, so the agency did not want me to adopt him. When his case manager found out what had happened, we had to appear in court to discuss how to manage the escalation in his behavior. The judge decided that he should be placed in a group home, where he would be supervised by several adults. He still visited me on weekends and holidays, but he no longer lived with me full time. The day after they had moved him, I was getting ready to go to school when his alarm for school went off. I collapsed into a puddle of tears. I missed him. I missed being his mom. Even though I had worked so hard at being a good mom and I had done a lot for him, I felt like a failure. It was a devastating time. I was divorced, with no financial help and I had lost the only experience I'd had of being a mother.

Bobby is now 40 years old. He lives on the opposite coast from me, but we keep in contact. He has a pretty good life. He struggles, but he has a good job, a girlfriend, and a son in elementary school. From what I can tell, he seems to be a very loving father. He wants to be the best dad he can be, because he never had a positive or loving father his entire life. He tells me I'm the only mom he has. He has thanked me for loving him and teaching him things. I will always love him as my son.

EVERY SITUATION IS unique, but when your family is torn apart by separation and divorce, the process is heart-wrenching. You may feel like you're alone and that no one understands. Finding guidance and support when your life has crumbled is critical to your mental and emotional health. You will find healing and the pain will lessen with time. You are holding a tool of hope and renewal in your hands right now. You will learn many powerful strategies that will help you rise from the rubble to create a life you may have never allowed yourself to dream of. Continue reading to receive inspiration from the stories of others who have had to completely start their lives over.

This is a short book, but it is jam-packed with proven strategies that, if practiced and applied, have the power to turn your sorrow into joy and your brokenness into wholeness. Chapter 1 begins with a message of hope. You will read the story of Sonia, a woman you may identify with in many ways. In Chapter 2, I share my story about the events that led to me leaving the life I'd known for 21 years, completely rebuilding, starting my life coaching business, and writing this book to help other women. In Chapter 3, you will learn about nurturing and caring for yourself, so you can become centered and find balance during a time when everything is upside-down. You will get very clear on what you most value and the vision you'd like to create for your life in Chapter 4. Chapter 5 will walk you through designing the life that will feed your soul and bring you joy. In Chapter 6, you will identify self-defeating thoughts that lead to self-defeating behaviors. You will learn ways to catch your negative thoughts and replace them with self-supporting ones. Chapter 7 will remind you how important it is to stay in gratitude. When you choose gratitude, your emotions stay more in check, and healing will come more quickly. Chapter 8 guides you through ways to strengthen your intuition. You will learn how to practice and increase your ability to tune into your higher self. In Chapter 9, I offer stories and strategies for speaking your truth. Chapter 10 urges you to keep pressing on, even in the face of fears and obstacles. Chapter 11 describes healing journeys you can take to build your confidence and face your fears. You can choose to take short or long adventures on your own or join me on one of the healing retreats that I offer.

My hope for you is that you will find wisdom, solace, and hope in these pages. From one woman to another, this is my gift to you so your heart can become whole and your spirit can soar.

ACKNOWLEDGMENTS

I AM BEYOND grateful to my family for always standing by me, loving me unconditionally, supporting my passion for life, and listening to my wild ideas. Thank you for teaching me life lessons with such strength and integrity. Your ongoing support, deep listening, and reaching out to me across long distances gave me the strength I needed to keep going when things got rough. Mom and Ralph, I love and appreciate you more than life itself.

And to Cathy, Danielle, Suzi, Suzanne, Paula, Sue, Cece, Cheryl, and the wise women who are my friends, neighbors, and powerful mentors, you have buoyed me up when my life was crumbling, helped me see the light, encouraged me without fail, and enabled me to be vulnerable with you in times of uncertainty. Thank you for always loving me, seeing my gifts when I couldn't, and for always cheering me on to take big risks and live life to the fullest.

To my assistant extraordinaire, Tammara, I only found you recently, but I feel like we've been friends for years. You are my champion. You are skilled, positive, and such an incredibly strong and kindhearted woman.

To my coworkers at Saddle Mountain Elementary and Lincoln Elementary, I learned so many important life lessons from you. Your dedication, courage, wisdom, and integrity through the challenges and great rewards of educating children inspire me. Serving as your school counselor helped mold me into the person I am today, and I will always hold you in high esteem. You remain in my heart always.

Finally, I must thank Dr. Angela Lauria and her staff at The Author Incubator, along with the wonderful authors in my cohort. This book, and the ones to follow, have been burning within me for years. You have provided the opportunity for me to write this love letter from my heart for the women whose lives will be enriched by it. You have inspired me to start a movement that will transform lives. This has been my dream for such a long time. You truly are heart-inspired dream makers!

CHAPTER 1

HEALING YOUR HEART – YOU ARE NOT ALONE

THERE IS NO doubt that divorce is painful. Losing your plans and dreams for the future is devastating. Even if your marriage was less than perfect, you knew what to expect. There was a predictability and sense of stability in your life. You were known as a couple and a family. You lived your life as a married woman; and everyone knew you in that context. You knew your role. You had routines and traditions that you shared as a family. You experienced times of joy and sadness together, then suddenly it ended and nothing in your life remained the same. You suddenly had to figure out how to live as a single woman. It's a disturbing and heart-wrenching realization.

I know the pain and loss. I have experienced betrayal. I have lost dreams of the future. I have been forced to give up on the role of being a wife and partner. It is extremely painful, but I'm here to tell you that *you will heal*. You possess great wisdom and strength. You have life experience and wisdom that will sustain you. You will begin again, and you will emerge strong and happy.

I believe in you, and I am here to pass on the skills and strategies that have helped me, and my clients, start over. I am here to share my heart with you, so you will have hope for a brighter future. Together, we can do this. Receiving support and encouragement is key to your renewal. You are a powerful woman with a mighty heart, and you will begin again, stronger than ever.

I wrote this book because I want you to know, from someone who's been there, that there is hope. As you read, imagine we are sitting together over a cup of coffee sharing our stories. We've both been hurt and have suffered disappointment. We've felt shame and sadness. Change is difficult, especially after the age of 50, but we are wise and resilient.

If you have felt paralyzed with sadness and disappointment, you will most likely identify with Sonia. I'd like to tell you some of her story:

She sat at her kitchen table, staring into her cup of coffee, trying to think of a good excuse to call in to work sick. Sonia honestly didn't feel like she could pull herself out of the chair. Every morning she went through the motions. She dragged herself out of bed, stumbled into the kitchen, and fought back the tears as the coffee brewed. Then she would plop down at the table and think to herself, "What has become of me? How can I get my life back on track?"

Sonia was married to Aaron for 32 years. She was a wife and mother for more than half her life. Sonia and Aaron didn't have great communication and his negative attitude sometimes drove her crazy. Occasionally, Aaron had an explosive temper. It could be very unpredictable, so Sonia was often on edge, wondering when something would happen that would cause him to explode. He didn't hit or threaten her, but he would yell and say hurtful things.

Throughout the years, Sonia determined that the role of wife suited her, and she thought she and Aaron were a pretty good team overall. She believed they had a special bond that couldn't be broken. They had raised 3 children, shared in decision-making, took vacations, had some great mutual friends and had weathered many challenging circumstances together. Aaron had been complimentary of Sonia and was proud of her accomplishments and her talents. Their sex life was okay. Sonia thought being intimate once a week was pretty good for a couple who'd been together for so long. Aaron was often difficult to connect with due to his moodiness, so Sonia didn't have a lot of romantic feelings for him. She thought that was the way most marriages were, and the predictability of their life together was comforting.

That was the status quo for Sonia until one day Aaron came home from work, obviously flustered. When she urged him to talk, he finally told her he didn't love her anymore, and he wanted a divorce. He refused to try to fix their relationship, to discuss it, or to go to marriage counseling. Sonia collapsed to the floor and sobbed, while Aaron packed some things and left. Just like that, Sonia's entire life as she'd known it, was over. The family gatherings, traditions, vacations, friends, and the daily routine of having coffee together, discussing the news, having meals together, and taking care of the house—all in the past.

So here she was, in her kitchen, alone and incredibly sad, barely able to move, her body heavy and her heart broken. She continually asked herself, "How will I ever be able to put the pieces of my life back together?" "When will I feel joy again?

You may identify with Sonia. Maybe you have been betrayed and abandoned by your partner, or you may have been the one who decided your marriage had to end. Either way, dreams have been lost, hearts have been broken, plans for the future no longer apply, and the suffering and grief can be debilitating. Losing a partner of many years and all the memories attached is like losing part of yourself. In fact, the person you were in that relationship, will no longer exist in the same way. Women often need to get in touch with who they are as a single person and imagining the future alone can be terrifying.

When you're in the grips of grief, friends and family may sympathize, but they seldom really understand what you're going through. Coming to a place of acceptance that life as you knew it is forever changed, can be a lengthy process. I want you to know that I've been through the fire, and I've emerged stronger than I ever thought possible. Pain is difficult, but it can also be a great catalyst for change. We are powerful women, and together we can build lives full of meaning. Joy is possible, even after divorce.

After my first disastrous marriage, I was afraid to try again. I didn't want to repeat the same mistakes. I spent a year living alone to get in touch with who I was as a woman outside of a relationship. I read a lot of self-help and relationship books and did a lot of journaling and soul-searching. Then in 1995, I fell in love with a smart, witty and charming man. We were both afraid of messing things up, so we didn't get married until 2003.

But in the fall of 2015, my life fell completely apart. My marriage had been shaky for quite some time. Then I broke my wrist badly and felt very alone in my pain. Just 1 month later, my mom had a psychotic break at the age of 81. She was paranoid and delusional and began wasting away. While I was caring for my mom, I realized that she had fallen into a personal hell, because she had never had a voice of her own, and she didn't know how to put herself first or practice self-care. She lived for everyone else and sacrificed herself to live up to the expectations of others. It occurred to me that I could be looking at myself in 30 years if I didn't make some major changes in my life!

My mom's illness was a wake-up call for me. I had been hoping that my marriage would improve. I wanted us to find our way back to each other, but the tension and lack of peace I had been feeling for a long time had taken an emotional and physical toll on me. It became very clear that I needed to do what my mom had not done. I needed to have a voice and speak my truth. I had been living on edge for far too long. I was no longer willing to sacrifice myself by remaining in a situation that was causing me a great deal of pain and anxiety. I had to find peace for myself, even if it meant leaving everything I had dedicated myself to for so long.

When the situation continued to escalate, I made the agonizing decision to leave my 21-year relationship. I needed to find a way to crawl out of the rubble and pick up the pieces of my life, for the second time. I've since rebuilt my life on my own terms and I'm happy. I know you can be too. I've found my way back to my authentic self and I'm living according to my soul's purpose. Walk with me and you'll find your way back too.

DIVORCE IS LIKE A DEATH

WHEN YOUR MARRIAGE ends, it really is like suffering a death. Your foundation has crumbled and your life is in ruins. When your life falls apart, you lose your former identity. You were the wife who fulfilled her role by compromising, accommodating, and responding to your partner's needs. Then suddenly the person you were no longer exists and you are left feeling like an empty shell.

Though divorce is painful and feels completely devastating, you certainly are not alone. The principles in this book represent the strategies that helped me find my way back to peace. I want to emphasize that everyone is on their own personal journey. No one can tell you when, or if, it's time to leave. These tools apply equally as well if you are working to improve your relationship. If you follow the steps outlined, and apply what you've learned, you will be able to manage your emotions better, tune in to your intuition, calm yourself, speak your truth, seek support, and ultimately make the decision that is best for you.

I really believe that it's important that you follow your heart, and don't push yourself to make decisions about your relationship too quickly. I am greatly in favor of marriage. Having a loving, supportive relationship with someone you trust and with whom you can completely be yourself, is invaluable. If your partner is willing to try, and you wish to save your marriage, I believe you should give it everything you've got. Relationships can be very challenging. Do everything in your power to speak your truth, be grateful for the things that are working, and act and make decisions from a place of love. My heart goes out to you. I wish you love, joy, and peace.

Below, you will find a list of questions to ponder if you're unsure of whether you should leave your marriage. I purposely have not created a scoring system or commentary about the significance of your answers to these questions. Every relationship has it's own unique set of circumstances. No one outside the marriage can truly know what the best decision will be for you.

Before reading the questions, take three slow deep breaths in and out, drop into your heart, and ask for guidance. As you read each question, notice how your body feels as you sit quietly, allowing it to sink into your heart. If you feel resistance or fear, breathe into it and try to determine it's source. It can help greatly to journal about the reactions you have to each question, being as truthful with yourself as you can. You do not need to feel pressured to decide anything. This is a self-awareness tool for you. Utilize it if you feel it applies. If you feel you need support, talk it through with someone you trust. But the ultimate decision you make must come from your own heart.

Questions to ponder if you are considering leaving your marriage:

1. Have you begun to talk to friends and family about the challenges you're having in your marriage?

2. Do you often find yourself criticizing (or wanting to criticize) your partner, privately or in front of others?
3. Does your partner often criticize you, in private or public?
4. Do you believe your health is being affected negatively by the stress in your marriage?
5. Have you tried every communication method you can think of, to no avail?
6. Do you feel that your life is in constant turmoil, with miscommunication, arguments, fights, tension, and so on?
7. Do you often fantasize about living alone?
8. Do you feel obsessed with your unhappiness?
9. Do you feel anger overcoming you daily or almost daily?
10. Are you socially isolated because your partner doesn't get along with others?
11. Does your partner prevent you from building friendships or spending time with your family?
12. Has the intimacy been gone out of your marriage for more than six months?
13. Do you worry that your partner might physically harm you?
14. Are you or your partner experiencing bouts of explosive anger on a regular basis?
15. Do you feel you're being verbally or physically abused?
16. Does it seem to be more painful to stay in your marriage than it does to leave?

17. If you had all the resources you needed, would you leave right away?
18. Have you or your partner threatened to leave several times already?
19. Have you told a friend or family member that you're planning to leave?
20. Are you and your partner like strangers living in the same house, not talking, touching, or doing things together?
21. Has there been unresolved infidelity in your marriage?
22. Is your partner abusing substances or alcohol and refusing to get help?
23. Have you sought counseling or attended marriage seminars without seeing results?
24. When you or your partner arrive home, do you feel a sense of dread?
25. Is sleeping next to your partner emotionally painful?

If this exercise feels very difficult and emotional for you, I recommend that you take some time for self-care. Get away, go for a walk, or call someone you trust. Be good to yourself and take all the time you need.

THERE IS HOPE FOR HEALING

YOU MAY BE feeling raw pain right now. This is a very difficult place to be. With support and guidance, you will find the courage to move forward. This simple, yet powerful, system will walk you through very specific steps to enable you to rebuild a life of meaning and direction. You will find joy again!

Since you are reading this right now, I know that you are reaching for a lifeline. You need to see light in the darkness. Struggling through each day in a fog with a heavy heart is exhausting. Fighting back tears all day takes a toll. As if that weren't enough, if you've been telling friends and family how miserable you are, sometimes they begin pulling away, leaving you feeling even more alone and desperate than ever.

You need to know you can heal and live happily and fulfilled once again. I assure you that you can, and if you commit to working through this entire book, and choose to invest in your own transformation, you will find clarity and joy. You will become clear on what you value, what kinds of activities and goals you can get excited about, and how you can attain them.

This is my gift to you. I have wanted to share my story for a very long time to give women hope for a renewed life. As a woman, you possess great strength and resilience. You will be working through steps I have taken myself. You will work through this system alongside women I'm currently coaching. Together, we form a tribe of support and empowerment. By purchasing this book, you are now a member of that private community of support. Just go to my private Facebook page entitled, "Unbreakable Women Private Community," and enter the code "BOOK" when you are asked why you wish to join the group. You will be added to a community of women you can share with, lean on, and learn from.

CHAPTER 2

THE JOURNEY BEGINS

Owning our story and loving ourselves through that process is the bravest thing that we'll ever do.

—Brené Brown

WHEN I FIRST began making plans to leave my marriage, I had no idea where to begin. When the time came, I was prepared to live almost anywhere. The many decisions I had to make were absolutely terrifying! I spent many nights lying in bed, wide awake, with no idea what the future would hold. A black abyss loomed in front of me and I was forced to step off the edge.

As I considered the only options I could come up with, renting a bedroom or living in an apartment with college students, I was paralyzed with fear. But I have a strong belief that when something is right, doors open. I waited and trusted with great trepidation.

I'd like to pause here to say that action is necessary for synchronicity to occur. I had no idea how things would work out, so I trusted, but I also took steps forward. I had heard about a community where home prices and rentals were much more reasonable than the homes near the university, so I went there to look around.

Soon after that, the magic began to unfold. I was driving around with a friend, and we passed a house that had a "For Sale by Owner" sign on it. My friend, Cathy, said, "Let's go see it!" and I said, "I can't afford a whole house!" She convinced me to stop just for fun. When I told the owner my story, he asked, "How much can you afford per month?" I told him, "$650," half the price of rentals in town. Amazingly, he volunteered to carry the contract for me.

Being able to secure that house was a miracle! It was just the miracle I needed. If, however, I had *not* had that door open for me, I would have rented a room and created a sacred space of my own. I was very fortunate to find a house to live in, but either way I would have made it work. Two weeks later I moved into my new home.

When you're going through pain, it's very difficult to make any kind of decision effectively. The first concept you will learn about and practice is self-care. It's absolutely crucial to have this piece in place, so you can have the strength and resolve to move forward. So many women have a tendency to put self-care last.

I also cannot stress enough the importance of surrounding yourself with supportive people. Being part of a tribe you can rely on is incredibly powerful. If you don't have a tribe of your own, you will have the chance to join the women on Facebook who have also read this book, as well as those who have worked directly with me. My signature group coaching program is called "Unbreakable Women with Courageous Hearts." The name is inspired by a song by a Canadian singer, Coco

Love Alcorn, called "Unbreakable," that I play at my live events. It's a powerful and uplifting song.

Once you are taking care of yourself adequately, you'll gain the clarity necessary to begin discovering what you really value and what your personal priorities are. This will enable you to create a vision for your future, so you can begin to think about the life you would like to design on your own terms. This takes time, and it's incredibly important that you are good to yourself and allow your heart to heal while you go through this process. You will work through a very powerful values clarification exercise in Chapter 4 that will bring you clarity and direction.

WHEN I FIRST met my client, Darcy, she had just left a very toxic relationship. Her self-esteem and confidence were at an all-time low. She had always lived for her husband and children, and had great difficulty figuring out what she wanted in her life as a single woman. She began using the techniques you will learn in this book. Darcy found herself getting clearer on details about who she wanted to spend time with, where she wanted to live, and what type of environment she wanted to create for herself.

When you are in the midst of making major life changes, it will help you immensely to align your thoughts with your desires. As you work through the chapters and begin to get clarity for creating a new life on your terms, you will be able to direct your thoughts to fulfill your dreams. Learning ways to consistently choose self-supporting thoughts over self-sabotaging ones will ensure your success and increase your self-confidence.

When things fell apart for me, my motto became, "No more at 54." It had taken me this long to decide I would live for *me*, on my own terms. I knew I had to stop stuffing my thoughts and feelings. Women are caregivers and natural nurturers, and in the process of making sacrifices for others, we often accommodate to the point of ignoring our own needs. We say, "yes" to things we don't feel good about. We push our feelings and needs aside. This is why learning to speak your truth with an authentic voice is so important. Stuffing and denying your emotions can accumulate to the point of making you sick. Don't you think it's about time that you became empowered to speak the truth that is in your heart?

You will get clarity as you heal. You will begin designing a life that emerges from your very soul. This is possibly something you've never had the opportunity to do before, but now you are free to design the life of your dreams, on *your* terms, for *your* happiness. While you are healing, growing, creating, and learning to put yourself first, practicing gratitude daily will keep your heart and mind in an uplifted state, and provide a net for you when obstacles arise.

While I was in the process of changing my life and also advocating for my mom's care, the one thing that anchored me was living in gratitude. I hadn't been sleeping well. Tears would randomly flow down my cheeks throughout the day, and I had become weary of trying to come up with an "acceptable" answer when colleagues asked, "How are you?" I clearly remember walking to work one day, with my knees wobbling, my stomach in knots, and my throat aching from trying to hold back the tears. I looked up at a tree that had several robins sitting on the branches, singing away. I paused to listen to their sweet song and said, "Thank you." I didn't have much to hang on to, but just pausing to be grateful for that one moment of beauty uplifted me.

Once you begin making decisions and taking steps forward, tuning in to your personal GPS system will give you the guidance and direction you long for. Your higher self, God, Spirit, the Universe, or whatever you choose to call it, knows the answers. You will practice tuning into your sixth sense and trusting it. You will be amazed at the synchronicities that will occur and the messages you will receive.

As you learn to trust your gut, follow the signs, and gain confidence in yourself, you will be ready to start overcoming fears and taking risks. You can start small and build up your courage. In time, if you keep facing fears and stepping into the unknown, you will learn that you are capable of so much more than you thought possible. You are a mighty woman with a powerful heart!

The last chapter will describe the healing journey I took during the summer of 2016. Here you will learn about opportunities to do this with me in a group of like-minded women, if you choose to heal your pain more quickly. Or you may decide to take a healing pilgrimage of your own. It's one of the most rewarding experiences you'll ever have, and I guarantee it will change your life!

Each chapter builds on the previous one, but you are free to skip around if you choose. My hope for you is that you will commit to completing the activities, and choose to finish the entire book. You are making an investment in yourself and your future. We are embarking on this journey together and together we will rise victorious.

CHAPTER 3
STEP 1: SELF-CARE TOOLBOX FOR HEALING

Self-compassion is simply giving the same kindness to ourselves that we would give to others.

—CHRISTOPHER GERMER

WHEN MY CLIENT, Jasmine, came to me, she wasn't sleeping well. She was agonizing over her feelings of failure, and she was deeply depressed. Negative thoughts were relentlessly playing in her head. She felt so exhausted and defeated that she was barely able to accomplish basic daily tasks. Together, we decided to start with small steps to help her build some self-care into each day. She was resistant at first, because she felt so worthless. However, Jasmine was extremely tired of feeling miserable, so she committed to giving it a try.

Jasmine chose two activities. Music had always been important to her, so she decided to create a playlist of 10–20 uplifting songs. Since she hadn't been doing much physical activity at all, she decided she would listen to her playlist while walking around her neighborhood. The next time I saw her, Jasmine looked brighter and was thinking more clearly. She was still struggling with feeling sad, but she was beginning to feel some hope for her future. She then decided to create a sacred space for herself in her bedroom. Each night she listened to Tibetan singing bowls to soothe herself.

WE ALL NEED ways to comfort and calm ourselves. But when we become adults, we often abandon this practice of self-soothing. We push ourselves to exhaustion, and we're reluctant to ask for help. We become anxious, stressed, and depressed, but we press on and wonder why our nervous systems become frazzled. We seldom give our bodies the opportunity to recover from the onslaught of stimulation and defeating thoughts.

I'd like to share the self-care techniques with you that I provide for my clients. They will provide a solid foundation for you as you begin to move forward. I've discovered techniques that will help you get through difficult times. I'm going to reveal several strategies for you to choose from to create a "self-care toolbox" that you can refer to daily to nurture and calm yourself. When waves of pain or grief hit you, your heart shuts down and you can't think clearly. I've placed self-care at the beginning, because you can't make decisions and create a future for yourself, if you're not first taking care of yourself. You will be able to choose activities that you decide will be most effective for you. Then when those dark times envelop you, you'll have your choices to draw from when you're unable to think clearly.

CREATING A SACRED SPACE

WHEN I WAS 5 or 6, I created a special place in my closet. I sat with my favorite blanket wrapped around me, with stuffed animals beside me, and my favorite book in hand. I snacked on lemon cooler cookies while I read. I felt safe and comforted in my cocoon-like spot. It was the first sacred place I ever created.

What about you? Did you have a closet sanctuary? A tree house? Did you love making blanket forts under a table? These are examples of naturally calming spaces that we created for ourselves as children. Can you remember how soothing and magical it felt? My loft in my tiny home is my sacred space now. It's a very comforting place to be.

Creating a sacred space in your home is a powerful first step in self-care. It's a daily reminder that you are putting yourself first for a change. Include items that are meaningful to you. You can collect things from nature, such as stones, driftwood, plants, feathers, leaves, or other items that have textures and colors you enjoy. You can also include family heirlooms, photos, religious symbols, fabric, and anything else that brings you joy. You might even include your journal or a favorite book.

I use my grandmother's antique table to display comforting items. I have favorite polished stones, a cross, a family photo, a large seashell, a Depression glass bowl from my mother, and a deck of cards with uplifting quotes by Dr. Wayne Dyer. Whenever I need to calm down, focus, or get centered, I spend time in my sacred space.

Do you have a space that feels sacred to you? If not, what types of objects, colors, textures, and mementos are soothing and calming for you? Which items represent something about who you are at your core? What helps you feel grounded? When you have created your very own sacred space, post a photo on the private Facebook page to share with other women. We will all benefit from seeing your creation.

Self-care is something that must become a conscious choice. When I was working as a counselor for 20 years and helping families cope with devastating tragedies, I would often arrive home feeling sad and almost completely numb. When I could barely think straight, I had a list of rituals and activities I could choose from to nurture and revive myself. One of my favorite self-healing rituals was to take a hot bath with Epsom salts and lavender oil. I would turn out the bathroom lights, light an aromatherapy candle, and meditate with a video from YouTube or music from my personal collection.

What soothes you? What personal items touch your heart? What types of objects help you feel grounded? Gather together some special things right now in a space in your home that can be dedicated to *you*. Choose a place that is private, where you will not be disturbed. If you do not have very many things to choose from, brainstorm some objects you'd like to collect for your space, and then begin creating it. This is a powerful step to take toward your healing.

EMOTIONAL SUPPORT

ANOTHER CRUCIAL FORM of self-care is having people in your life who are willing to listen deeply, support you, and offer encouragement. If someone drains your energy, guard your heart by choosing to look to someone else for emotional support. When my life was falling apart and I was in tears at random times throughout the day, I had a few friends I could call on. I could not have made it through that devastating time without their love and support. The feelings I was experiencing were intense, so I alternated between friends. I didn't want to add stress to their lives or take too much time away from their jobs and families. I also reached out to family members I hadn't talked to in a long time. We were able to reconnect in a powerful way, and having that foundation shored me up in ways I never expected.

Who do you have to talk to? Make a list of people who you feel supported by and loved just as you are. If your circumstances have caused people to pull away, go on Facebook and share your thoughts and feelings. If you ask, chances are you will find a special sharing partner you can speak with offline, as well.

If you don't have anyone to talk to and you are severely depressed, anxious, or suicidal, you can call the National Crisis Line any time of the day or night at 1-800-273-8255. You can also text "ANSWER" to 839863, and someone will text you back. There is no shame in needing support. We all have times when it feels as though our entire foundation has been pulled out from under us. If you are alone, and need to talk to someone, call or text this number. Give yourself the gift of support from a trained professional, free of cost.

If you want to make new friends, attend community events, participate in Meetup groups, attend church or volunteer.

If you are unable to find a group that suits you, sign up to be a host on meetup.com and create your own book club or group.

LOVING YOURSELF

WE ARE TOLD to love ourselves and to put our oxygen mask on first, so we can help others. However, we are incredibly hard on ourselves and leave our needs for last. We are quick to criticize ourselves and practice all kinds of self-defeating behaviors. Additionally, the mixed messages thrown at women can make our heads spin. We're seen as too smart and therefore arrogant, or we're not smart enough and are labeled as "ditzy". We're judged as too thin, or too heavy, or somehow just not quite right. We need to speak up, but then we're too brash. We are supposed to dress professionally and show our power, but if we do, we might be labeled as "pushy" or "bitchy." The list goes on and on. Is it any wonder that eating disorders, anxiety, and depression are on the rise? We seek love outside of ourselves and we feel unworthy of unconditional love. Learning to love ourselves is a process. It takes awareness of the critical tapes we play in our heads, and it takes commitment to begin replacing them, while we seek ways to be proud of ourselves.

Lisa Nichols, an incredibly dynamic inspirational speaker, has an exercise she asks her students to do called

Mirror Work. You begin every day by looking into the mirror, deep into your own eyes, and saying, "I love you," "I forgive you," and "I'm proud of you." Each day you add things that you love about yourself, forgive yourself for, and are proud of. This can be a difficult exercise, because it brings your greatest insecurities to the surface. But if you commit to doing this, you will be amazed at the things that come up for you. Yes, it can be challenging, but you will also receive great healing from it. Journaling about this experience will help you assimilate the powerful lessons you learn and having a "mirror work buddy" will further enhance the experience. You can find Lisa Nichols on YouTube and she offers online courses through Mindvalley.com.

RECOGNIZE YOUR TALENTS AND GIFTS

ANOTHER EXERCISE THAT will help you is to create a timeline of major events that have occurred in your entire life, and then list the knowledge and skills you acquired as a result of those experiences. We often forget how many incredible skills we possess. Look at the occurrences in your life and the lessons you learned from those times, whether they were accomplishments or major challenges. Spend some time on this and make it fun by using colored pens, stickers, or pictures cut out of magazines or printed off the internet.

When you encounter particularly painful memories, stop to get support if you feel yourself getting triggered. You can always put that memory on hold for now, until you get stronger. Once you've completed your timeline, you can utilize a method I call, "Rewriting Your Story." In my signature group-coaching program, at the live event, we craft our personal stories so they can help others who have similar challenges. The key is to transform a story that was formerly focused on victimization, into one of resilience. If you have survived trauma, or abuse, or any trying circumstances, you are a survivor, and you have great strength and resolve within you. Take a moment right now to identify the attributes you had to possess in order to survive. Just for starters, you most certainly learned to read subtleties in the behavior of others. You had to be very alert and tuned in to survive. Chances are you learned to be very resourceful to protect yourself. You had to have "mental toughness". You most likely became very hypervigilant so you could detect the slightest changes in your environment. You may have become highly skilled at self-soothing. What other traits did you develop? It's important to recognize the unique strengths you developed in response to your particular circumstances.

> *"You can recognize survivors of abuse by their courage. When silence is so very inviting, they step forward and share their truth so others know they aren't alone."*
>
> —JEANNE MCELVANEY

GETTING YOUR NATURE FIX

I CANNOT EMPHASIZE enough how healing it is to give yourself time in nature. The Environmental Protection

Agency estimates that the average American spends 93% of their time indoors. Nature is incredibly calming and renewing, and we really must make a conscious effort to get outdoors whenever we can. Spend at least a few minutes every day walking in nature. This might mean walking in a forest, by a lake or river, or just going into your backyard. Using all five senses, take the time to soak in your surroundings completely. Listen, touch, feel, smell, and observe, while breathing deeply in and out. This allows your brain to rest from the constant swirling thoughts. It is a sort of walking meditation that is very calming. Gift yourself with this very simple but powerful technique. Allow the miracle of nature to rejuvenate your spirit.

I was doing this long before I heard of the term, "forest bathing," which began in Japan and is referred to as *Shinrin-yoku*. If you'd like to know more about this amazing practice, you can read the book, *Forest Bathing*, by Dr. Qing Li.

ANTICIPATION

ANOTHER POWERFUL MOTIVATOR and method that increases happiness, is to have things to look forward to. If you are struggling with lethargy and feeling numb or incredibly sad, find something every day that you can look forward to, and follow through with this commitment to yourself. You might decide to incorporate any of the methods listed in this chapter as special gifts to yourself, or you might supplement with something you particularly love to do. Perhaps you'll buy special bath salts or a new candle, so you can take a luxurious bath. You may download a song to dance to, or reward yourself by watching your favorite show on Netflix. Or maybe you'll drive home from work via a different route, so you can stop somewhere to walk in nature. Whatever you decide to do, find something you can gift yourself with and anticipate every day. This can improve your mood greatly and will serve as a constant reminder that you are taking care of yourself.

JOYFUL DISCOVERIES

JOY IS AN emotion that bubbles up within us when something surprises and thrills us. Happiness is more of a consistent state that we experience by choice. We have the choice of finding things to be happy about, often by feeling gratitude for the things we decide to appreciate in our lives. But joy is something that happens in a moment and often comes by surprise. A toddler might run up to you, put his hands on your legs and grin widely. You may see a puppy waddling down the sidewalk. Maybe a good friend calls and says they are coming to visit. These are unexpected occurrences that bring joy. The key to discovering joy on a regular basis, leading to more sustained happiness, comes from looking for reasons to be joyful.

We often spend so much time in our heads that the world essentially passes us by. A technique I like to practice is one I call, "Right Now." I use this to bring my awareness into the moment. Instead of thinking about the past or planning for the future, I remind myself, "Right now, I am in this moment," so I can experience what is actually happening. Here's how this works; instead of sitting in the coffee shop, for example, staring at my phone and checking my email, I stop and look at my surroundings. I notice the people who are present, listen to the music playing, and look at the scenery outside. When I become aware, I notice things that bring me joy. I would miss those wonderful sparks of inspiration if I continued being lost in my thoughts.

Here's another example of how to use Right Now. When I go for a walk, I work on staying out of my head, so I can completely experience my surroundings. I tell myself, "Right now, I am listening to the birds sing. I am enjoying the blue sky. I'm watching the sun bounce off the water. I'm listening to the rustling of the leaves, and enjoying the intricate beauty of the flowers." This can be another form of walking meditation that puts you in touch with endless sources of joy. There is a great Ted Talk on this subject by Ingrid Fetell Lee entitled, "Where Joy Hides and How to Find It." You can find it on YouTube.

MANAGING EMOTIONS

EMOTIONS CAN BE intense and debilitating. Sometimes all it takes is a smell or sound to trigger a painful memory, and the sadness creeps in like an uninvited guest. Waves of grief can overtake you and make you feel like you're drowning. Anger can embed itself in your very core and take root.

When I feel that familiar heaviness in my chest and the gnawing in my stomach, it helps me a great deal to remember that feelings are like clouds. They may appear large and dark, but they do pass. Just the knowledge that they are temporary helps to dissipate the fear that can accompany such strong emotions. It's also very empowering to learn to sit with your emotions, because for many of us, our first instinct is to avoid or stuff them.

If you teach yourself to stay with a feeling, breathe into it, and comfort yourself with supportive thoughts, just like you'd comfort a child or dear friend, you will gain the satisfaction of having control. When you learn that you can manage the emotions that arise throughout the day in this way, you will feel much more confident. This will also enable you to eliminate some of the self-sabotaging behaviors you may have developed to escape the difficult sensations of these feelings.

I have found a process that helps me greatly when negative feelings overtake me. As soon as I notice the tightness in my neck and shoulders, and restriction in my breathing, I stop what I'm doing. I first try to determine what I had been thinking that may have contributed to these feelings creeping in. Then if I can't break the pattern by breathing and releasing the emotions, I immediately engage in a different activity. I prefer to spend time outside because it clears my head and helps me break out of the negative loop. When I go outside, I engage all my senses to stop the swirling thoughts in my mind. I look at the sky, smell the air, feel plants or trees, listen to the birds and allow my nervous system to become balanced and calm again. Then, after I've walked around and taken several deep breaths, I return home and call someone. This is the best way I've found to break the pattern of stress and anxiety. If I don't have someone to call, I type or write in my journal to get everything out. I am then able to identify the thoughts and concerns that had piled up and caused me to go into fear.

You may experience times when your emotions accumulate to the point where you feel paralyzed. It feels like they swallow you and you can't think clearly enough to calm yourself. In my experience, when this occurs, you are operating from a place of fear. The amygdala in your brain becomes overactive, and you are thrown into a state of fight, flight, or freeze. It can happen rather quickly, catching you off guard. It may even become or resemble a panic attack. Your chest tightens, your breathing is shallow, your heart pounds, and you feel like running or hiding. When you recognize you're in this state, stop what you're doing and take a sensory break. This helps to break your nervous system out of fear.

In Chapter 6, you will learn about the connection between your thoughts and emotions, and you'll learn how to gain control over continuous self-destructive loops. By practicing these skills, you will be well on your way to taking control of your life, and you will be laying a solid foundation for your future.

REFRAMING PAINFUL MEMORIES

In Neurolinguistic Programming (NLP), there is a powerful and fun technique that I have found to be very helpful. If you can envision pictures and scenes in your mind, you should be able to do this exercise with ease. Find a quiet, peaceful location where you will not be disturbed. Sit comfortably and close your eyes. Breathe deeply, through your nose, into your belly and out through your mouth several times. Allow any stress to melt away. Envision a painful scene that you have been replaying over and over in your mind, but picture it in black and white.

Watch the scene from a distance, as if you're viewing a movie. Continue breathing as you keep yourself out of the emotion of the scene. When you feel ready, begin to change the scene in your mind to an outcome you wish you'd had. For example, if you were yelled at and belittled, but were unable to defend yourself, change the scene to one in which you stood up for yourself and remained safe.

As you change the scene to a more positive outcome, add color back into it. Feel the victimization and humiliation dissolve. Then as the scene becomes colorful and full of life, add a song to it that is uplifting for you. One of my favorites is "The Fight Song" by Rachel Platten. Make sure to use a song that evokes a feeling of empowerment. Once you have created this scene for yourself, breathe deeply and open your eyes.

Now, if any negative track tries to play in your mind, you can erase the emotional charge of it by letting the memory fade to black and white, then empower yourself with the new colorized version. Your brain will grab onto this new memory, if you let yourself envision it again and again. Your brain does not differentiate between reality and fantasy when it comes to what you think about and envision. This is a fabulous healing tool.

CHILL WITH CREATIVITY

NEVER UNDERESTIMATE THE power of applying creativity toward healing. Creativity is immensely calming and healing. If you don't feel artistic, that's okay. It really doesn't matter. Think back to your childhood to creative activities that brought you joy. Did you love sculpting clay? Were you a master at doodling? Did you love to cook or bake? Did you do beadwork? Perhaps you enjoyed needlepoint or knitting. Maybe you just loved to color. There are a multitude of adult coloring books for a reason; they are a very effective means of getting calm and centered.

When I first left my marriage, I found that painting rocks was very soothing. I am not an accomplished painter, by any means, but I enjoyed getting ideas from YouTube and Pinterest. I gave my creations to friends, and sometimes left them for someone to find. I also felt the urge to start making jewelry and bookmarks with beads. I really enjoyed doing this for a while. As I healed and began to make plans for my future, according to my values-based vision (that you'll be learning about next), I found that I no longer had the urge to do these projects.

Other forms of creative expression include writing, decorating, sending special cards to friends and family, or using software programs to make designs. Incorporating music into any creative endeavor makes it that much more enjoyable. Music is a lifeline for me. I have several playlists that I've compiled for inspiration and encouragement. Sometimes I walk or ride while listening to my music. Other times I just dance at home.

Which songs lift you to a higher place? Make a playlist so you can take advantage of their power when you need it.

I'm sure you have your own special self-care strategies that work well for you. Feel free to share your favorite ways of nurturing yourself on the Facebook page. Others will benefit greatly from your input.

Choose at least five techniques from this chapter that you can use whenever you are in pain, feel out of sorts, or just need a lift. Write them down in your journal or post the list where you'll see it every day. Label the list, "Self-Care Toolbox." The best way to make sure you are regularly engaging in self-supporting activities is to schedule them. Use the calendar on your phone to assign one method to each day. You might schedule music and dancing on Monday. Then you might do creative activities such as drawing, painting or working in your garden on Tuesdays, and so on, for the entire week. Putting yourself first and caring for yourself in this way, will greatly enhance the effectiveness of the other strategies. You are beginning to rebuild your life with strength and clarity. If you prefer a large list of choices at your fingertips, you can download a free self-care checklist from my website at www.MidlifeRenewalCoach.com. The checklist can be posted in a prominent place in your home or at work, so you can see all the choices you have for scheduling self-care strategies into each day.

CREATE A COMMUNITY OF SUPPORT

FOR MANY WOMEN, getting divorced might also lead to losing mutual friends. People can become subconsciously fearful that divorce is somehow contagious. Some people are uncomfortable with the thought that they might need to "choose sides," so they avoid their former friends altogether. It's devastating to lose your support network.

As I mentioned previously, you can receive support from our wonderful online community. But you'll also need to make new friends. Meetup groups in your area can be a great way to get to know new people. Find a group that's devoted to activities you enjoy. You can find coffee groups, hiking or walking groups, singles groups, crafting groups, book clubs, and many more. Search on meetup.com to find groups in your area. You can also attend church, participate in community events, or volunteer. Do some research, identify something you'd like to do, and set a goal for yourself to engage in one new activity each month. You will not regret creating the opportunity to make new friends.

In the next chapter, you will identify the things you value most, and you will begin to create a plan for your future. While you're identifying the life you wish to create for yourself, it's imperative that you continue to practice self-care on a daily basis.

CHAPTER 4

STEP 2: CREATE YOUR VALUES-BASED VISION

*Living with integrity means behaving in ways
that are in harmony with your personal values.*

—BARBARA DE ANGELIS

M Y CLIENT, CATRINA, grew up with an abusive stepfather. She was trapped in a situation that filled her with fear, shame, and anger. She went from an abusive childhood into an abusive marriage. Catrina perfected the skill of adapting who she was to survive. When her husband went to prison for assaulting a coworker, Catrina was left feeling like an empty shell. She had spent her entire life succumbing to the control of others. Catrina did not have an identity of her own.

As we worked together, she began to identify the many skills she had acquired to overcome her challenging circumstances. Catrina was resourceful, resilient, intuitive, and highly skilled at reading people's character and emotions. When Catrina was alone, she wrote beautifully poignant poetry and turned her poetry into songs.

She was able to use her skills of seeing subtleties and reading people to capture incredible photos.

When she worked through the values clarification exercise, Catrina ended up choosing the core value of Beauty. She made the conscious choice to continually see beauty in her surrounding world, and to capture that beauty to share with others. She now creates and sells gorgeous montages of photography and poetry that flow from her heart.

How about you? Are you aware of what you value most? Do you base your daily decisions on what really matters to you? Are you able to identify what makes your heart sing and your spirit soar? Defining your values helps you to set priorities and to get very clear on how you'd like your life to proceed. When you know exactly what to live for, you stop wasting time. You won't struggle so much with procrastination. You'll say "no" to soul-draining activities and you'll know exactly what to say "yes" to.

You may decide that at this time in your life, you want to choose to work on having more courage and taking more risks. You may decide that you'd like to teach others some of the things you've learned thus far. When you identify what you enjoy most, you will also recognize your core values.

I have always valued honesty and integrity. Treating others with kindness and respect will always be at the heart of decisions I make. For several years my core value was "Service". However, when my life changed so drastically, it suddenly became very important to me to face my fears and overcome them. I suddenly had the urge to travel and explore. My core value then became "Courage". I left my career to build a business that would allow me to help women transform their lives, while incorporating travel into my coaching programs and live events. My greatest desire is to inspire others to live life to the fullest extent, and therefore my focus is now on "Inspiration".

When my client, Anna, left her relationship in her 50s, she felt a very strong pull to return to her home-town. She had been away for more than 30 years. She quit her job, sold excess belongings, and began making plans to move close to her family. She had to live with her brother while she was in transition, but this gave her the opportunity to begin creating the life she really wanted for herself. Anna chose the core value of "Truth" because she was finally speaking her truth and living from her heart.

When you complete this next exercise, you will become clear on what you value and you will then be able to create a vision for your new life.

VALUES-CLARIFICATION EXERCISE

HERE ARE THE steps for completing the following val-ues-clarification exercise. Read the explanation for each step about how to complete this exercise most thor-oughly and effectively. This will set you up with a clear foundation to build upon, when you begin designing the life you desire in the next chapter.

STEP 1

Take some time in a quiet space or in nature, and using a journal, brainstorm all of the engaging and inspirational activities you've done in your life.
Find a quiet spot in your sacred space or outside in nature. Take three slow deep breaths. Close your eyes and place your hand on your heart. Ask yourself what brought you the most joy in the past. Allow your thoughts to flow freely and give yourself as much time as you need. As things come to you, write them in your journal. Write down everything that comes to you, without worrying about whether they are "practical" or not.

Think back to your childhood. How did you prefer to spend your time? What brought you the most joy? What was so enthralling to you that it made you completely lose track of time?

STEP 2

Look at the alphabetical list of values below and circle any of the values that jump out at you.
Take your time; there's no need to rush. This will give you a strong foundation when you begin creating a personal design for your new life. This exercise is focused on giving you the space to heal and begin to think about what you'd like to create for yourself. It is a guide for you. There is no urgency. Take your time and keep checking in with your heart as you move forward. Nurture yourself and listen to the direction you receive from within.

When you feel ready, look over the list of values. Look over the entire list once. Then circle any of the values that feel especially important to you. Breathe deeply and allow your intuition to guide you.

STEP 3

Group the values you chose into related categories.
Next, go back through the values you circled. Notice if any of them fit into a category together. For example, Candor, Honesty, Truth, Honor, and Integrity are all related, so you might choose "Truth" to represent all of them.

STEP 4

Choose the value that best describes each category for you.

For each grouping, you can then choose the value that is most important for you. When you have chosen a main descriptor, underline that word:

STEP 5

Journal about each value word, free-writing about what each of the words mean to you.
After you've narrowed down the related groups of values, write each of the underlined words in your journal. Set aside 5–10 minutes to journal about each word. Set a timer and free-write without stopping. If writing is difficult for you, make an audio recording or dictate to someone you trust. Record what

that word means to you for your life going forward. Even if you don't see yourself as a writer, you will be amazed at how enlightening this activity is. This is for you and no one else. You don't need to have any concern for grammar, spelling, or how coherent the writing is. The point is to tap deeply into your consciousness to discover the hidden gems within.

STEP 6

Google a quote for each word and post the quotes where you will see them every day.

Search for a related quote, for each value word, that really represents your values. The quote that I live by for my value of "Courage" is, "She believed she could, so she did." I have this hanging in my bathroom on a wooden sign.

Find a quote that speaks to you and post it in a prominent place as a daily reminder. You might also buy jewelry to wear that has your word on it. I wear a necklace with my favorite quote engraved on it. I have one client that had her core value tattooed on the inside of her forearm, so she could be reminded constantly about what she stands for, and what she is basing her life decisions on.

STEP 7

Choose one primary value that will guide you in making decisions and setting priorities for this time in your life.

This is the primary value that rings loudest for you and describes what you most desire to present to the world. Your core value will guide you as you pick up the pieces to rebuild a life on your terms.

I want to leave a legacy of providing inspiration so others can fully express their inner greatness. What do you want to be remembered for? What is the legacy you'd like to leave for your family and friends?

It is in your moments of decision that your destiny is shaped.

—TONY ROBBINS

Here is the list of 230 personal values: (excerpt from ScottJeffrey.com)

Acceptance	Bravery	Community
Accomplishment	Brilliance	Compassion
Accountability	Calm	Competence
Accuracy	Candor	Concentration
Achievement	Capable	Confidence
Adaptability	Careful	Connection
Alertness	Certainty	Consciousness
Altruism	Challenge	Consistency
Ambition	Charity	Contentment
Amusement	Cleanliness	Contribution
Assertiveness	Clear	Control
Attentive	Clever	Conviction
Awareness	Comfort	Cooperation
Balance	Commitment	Courage
Beauty	Common sense	Courtesy
Boldness	Communication	Creation

Creativity	*Feelings*	*Inspiring*
Credibility	*Ferocious*	*Integrity*
Curiosity	*Fidelity*	*Intelligence*
Decisive	*Focus*	*Intensity*
Decisiveness	*Foresight*	*Intuitive*
Dedication	*Fortitude*	*Irreverent*
Dependability	*Freedom*	*Joy*
Determination	*Friendship*	*Justice*
Development	*Fun*	*Kindness*
Devotion	*Generosity*	*Knowledge*
Dignity	*Genius*	*Lawful*
Discipline	*Giving*	*Leadership*
Discovery	*Goodness*	*Learning*
Drive	*Grace*	*Liberty*
Effectiveness	*Gratitude*	*Logic*
Efficiency	*Greatness*	*Love*
Empathy	*Growth*	*Loyalty*
Empower	*Happiness*	*Mastery*
Endurance	*Hard work*	*Maturity*
Energy	*Harmony*	*Meaning*
Enjoyment	*Health*	*Moderation*
Enthusiasm	*Honesty*	*Motivation*
Equality	*Honor*	*Openness*
Ethical	*Hope*	*Optimism*
Excellence	*Humility*	*Order*
Experience	*Imagination*	*Organization*
Exploration	*Improvement*	*Originality*
Expressive	*Independence*	*Passion*
Fairness	*Individuality*	*Patience*
Family	*Innovation*	*Peace*
Famous	*Inquisitive*	*Performance*
Fearless	*Insightful*	*Persistence*

Playfulness	Sensitivity	Temperance
Poise	Serenity	Thankful
Potential	Service	Thorough
Power	Sharing	Thoughtful
Present	Significance	Timeliness
Productivity	Silence	Tolerance
Professionalism	Simplicity	Toughness
Prosperity	Sincerity	Traditional
Purpose	Skill	Tranquility
Quality	Skillfulness	Transparency
Realistic	Smart	Trust
Reason	Solitude	Trustworthy
Recognition	Spirit	Truth
Recreation	Spirituality	Understanding
Reflective	Spontaneous	Uniqueness
Respect	Stability	Unity
Responsibility	Status	Valor
Restraint	Stewardship	Victory
Results-oriented	Strength	Vigor
Reverence	Structure	Vision
Rigor	Success	Vitality
Risk	Support	Wealth
Satisfaction	Surprise	Welcoming
Security	Sustainability	Winning
Self-reliance	Talent	Wisdom
Selfless	Teamwork	Wonder

Please take all the time you need with this chapter. This is a foundational activity that will enable you to get the most value from the upcoming chapters. It's critical that you are clear on what you value most. When you begin designing the life you desire, and then begin to take steps toward starting over and transforming yourself and your life, your values will guide you every step of the way.

Although I highly recommend that you spend as much time as you need in this chapter, I want to caution you against getting stuck. If you have difficulty choosing your values, choose the ones that resonate most with you right now, and then keep moving forward. As you grow and heal, your values can change; this is not something that's carved in stone. This activity will bring you great clarity, but you can change your answers later. The most important thing you need to focus on right now is to continue learning and making progress. Everything will come together in time. Trust the process and, above all, trust yourself.

You will be carrying your personal values forward with you as you create your life design, learn to change your self-defeating thoughts into supportive ones, practice gratitude, and rely on your intuition. Everything will fall into place. Post your value word quotes so you can see them every day. Continue journaling about how you are making decisions based on your primary value. Write about what you'd like to do, and how you'd like your life to be, based on your foundational values. See it happening, believe it, and keep going! You can do this.

If you'd like to have a copy of the values list for yourself or for a book club, please go to my website for your free download.

CHAPTER 5

STEP 3: CREATE
YOUR LIFE DESIGN

*The best and most beautiful things in the world
cannot be seen or even touched—they must be
felt with the heart.*

—HELEN KELLER

YOU NOW HAVE a foundation to build upon that
reflects who you are and the desires you hold for the
new life you're creating. I hope you're feeling encouraged and hopeful. We are walking this journey together,
and I believe in you. I envision a bright future for you. I
hope you are beginning to see a bright light up ahead. I
trust that your heart is beginning to heal and open to
new possibilities. This system works if you are diligent in
staying with it. You have gotten this far in life because
you are strong and resilient. The treasures of who you
are and the purpose you're meant to fulfill lie within
your heart and soul. Let's sit down over a cup of coffee,
as you continue to move forward on your unique path.
Perhaps you'll be one of the incredible success stories
that I'll have the opportunity to share to encourage others!

Now that you have laid the bricks of your foundation with daily self-care and clarity of your core values, you are ready to begin designing the life you most desire to live. This could result in making some major changes, or it could lead to simply changing your perceptions and living your life with a renewed outlook. The ultimate outcome will be uniquely yours.

VISIONING YOUR NEW LIFE

To complete the following exercise most effectively, you will need to suspend judgments and thoughts of *how* you will create your ideal life design. This is just the beginning; a visioning process that will get the energy flowing in the direction of feeding your soul. This is meant to be a creative outlet unhampered by fear. View this as a fun, creative, heart-opening exercise to get your thoughts flowing. Do this as a gift to yourself. Share your final results with a friend if you like but complete the activity separately. That way you will not be influenced by anyone else's ideas or dreams. After you're done, feel free to post a photo of your creation on the Facebook page.

The focus of this chapter is on becoming very clear about all aspects of your new life. You can begin by being "far-fetched." It's important to dream big and to allow your spirit to take flight, without reservation. This will enable you to really unleash your creativity and let your desires flow freely. How often in life have you had the chance to "order," so-to-speak, anything and everything you ever wanted to have in your life? This is that chance. It's an exhilarating and empowering activity.

You have probably heard of creating a vision board toward manifesting your greatest desires. This is very similar and it is based on the same principles, but it is more detailed and specific for every area of your life. The first step is to write or type a narrative of the life you desire. If writing is difficult for you, create an audio recording or dictate to someone you trust. Take up to 30 minutes to develop your new story. Be sure to incorporate all the areas listed below. Write in present tense about your greatest dreams for your life. As before, write without stopping and without concern for the quality of your writing. Just get everything out on paper. Make sure you are feeling positive and strong enough emotionally, so that your creativity can flow freely. Put on some soothing music and sit in a comfortable space where you won't be disturbed. Write as if you are in your very own perfect story. For example, if I were writing mine, I might begin like this:

> *"I wake up in my canopy bed with my dogs happily sleeping on the floor beside me. The sun warms the room and makes the yellow walls glow. The pear tree outside my window is filled with robins and sparrows that greet me with their beautiful song. I walk into my blue and white kitchen with white tile floors and white quartz countertops. As I wait for my coffee to brew, I gaze out the large windows onto my deck, which overlooks the lake. I watch as a blue heron is standing like a statue, waiting for his breakfast. I sit on my deck in my red Adirondack chair with red and white cushions.*

*My deck is surrounded by flowering azaleas,
mums, and daisies...."*

Write your story without regard to what you think is
practical. I do not currently have this house on a lake,
but I believe I will someday. Just go with it.

PREPARE YOUR CREATIVE SPACE

YOU WILL BE creating your life design in the way that
speaks to you personally. You might cut pictures out
of magazines, or draw your vision, or take photos and
create a collage. Someone I know created a PowerPoint
slideshow with photos of each aspect of their life design.
You can check Pinterest for ideas, if you're not sure
which method you'd like to use. The key is to design
something that speaks to you, and gives a voice to the
desires that lie deep within you. You can also record a
video if you like, but I prefer something you can place in
your home that you will see every day.

You will be coming up with plans for all areas of your
life. These areas will overlap as you begin to put your
design together.

Life Design Components:

SOCIAL

> The social component includes such things as the
> types of people you want to surround yourself with,
> the activities you'd like to participate in, the way you
> want to feel in these social activities, the roles you'd

like to play, and the social events you might decide to create for yourself. Are there social groups you can join, such as civic groups, Meetup groups, church, or support groups? Or would you like to create your own group?

Work

Include the tasks you enjoy most, and those you'd like to include in your work day that you aren't doing now. Or perhaps you want to create a completely new experience for yourself; list the skills that you possess, and the types of activities that engage your heart and make you feel most alive. What type of environment would you prefer to work in? What types of personalities do you enjoy working with? Do you prefer to work independently or as part of a collaborative team? Have you always dreamt of starting your own business? Do you enjoy linear tasks that are clearly defined or more creative undefined tasks? What type of job will allow you to live out your core values and enable you to grow and shine? If you're retired, what do you enjoy doing that will enable you to continue learning and growing?

Physical

What do you enjoy doing to keep your body fit? Is there something you haven't tried yet that has always intrigued you? Where and how do you like to exercise, in nature, at home, at a gym, alone or with a friend? Are there social activities you can join to meet new friends and also get exercise, like dances, yoga, CrossFit, martial arts, rowing, kayaking, biking or hiking? Are there Meetup groups that focus on an activity you enjoy?

SPIRITUAL

How do you feed your soul? Do you have a spiritual practice? Do you attend group events or church? What are your core beliefs? What increases your faith? How do you prefer to seek guidance for your life? Are there spiritual teachings you've always wanted to know more about? Would you like to attend a spiritual retreat? Are there books you'd like to read to learn more? Are there workshops you'd like to attend?

HOME

What makes your home feel sacred and nourishing? Are there colors, textures, décor changes that would make your space more inviting? What type of home do you dream of living in? Where would you like your home to be located? What kind of environment do you picture your home in? For example, would you prefer to live in the city, in the woods, in the country, near the water, or on a hill? Do you dream of having a large home in which you can entertain? Or would you like a small, simple home that allows you the freedom to travel or be more involved in the community? Do you want a garden to work in? Would you like to have the space to have a pool or fire pit to invite friends to enjoy? What style and color do you prefer for your home, inside and out?

HOBBIES

What do you most enjoy doing in your spare time? Would you like to volunteer? If so, what would you like to do? Do you want to learn to do something you've never done before? Do you enjoy physical activities? Artistic endeavors? Travel? Include everything you can think of, knowing that you can always add more.

My client, Amy, found that creating a picture journal was what helped her the most. When she was feeling sad and depressed, she began collecting magazine pictures for the above categories. She pasted them into her journal and wrote thoughts and desires about them. She also added inspirational quotes and statements of gratitude. In less than a year, many of the dreams from her journal came true.

PLEASE SHARE YOUR life design creation in the private Facebook group. Take your time creating it and let this be an envisioning process that fills your heart with joy and anticipation of the life you're creating for yourself. I believe we attract what we focus on. You'll read more about this in the upcoming chapter.

In my own experience, things have happened for me that have no logical explanation. I thought about what I wanted, and I stayed in gratitude for what I already had. I envisioned my life coming together in very clear ways, and those things came to pass. Our visions do not always come quickly or without setbacks, and they may not unfold as we envisioned them. But in my experience, they work out in ways that are ultimately best for us. Continue with self-care and gratitude, so you can keep a good frame of mind, and keep your thoughts focused on your vision.

In the next chapter, you'll also learn about the importance of keeping your thoughts positive and self-supporting. The most important thing to remember is that having a clear vision, and then focusing on that, will enable the universe to conspire in your favor. I believe the universe, God, source energy, any way you choose to name it, supports us. Create your life design for each area in the most specific way you can. Then think about it, talk about it to friends and family, envision it happening, and don't allow doubt to creep in. Keep your eyes on the goal and you will see miraculous things occur in your life!

I look forward to seeing your personal creation on Facebook, and hearing about what this activity means to you, and how it has helped you.

CHAPTER 6

STEP 4: YOUR THOUGHTS CREATE YOUR REALITY

*We are born with this inner guidance, which
comes in the form of the emotions and desires
that lead us toward things (including thoughts)
that feel good and are good for us, and away
from things that feel bad and are bad for us.*

—CHRISTIANE NORTHRUP

THIS CHAPTER IS *the anchor* of this entire system for successfully rebuilding your life. When you can identify your sabotaging thoughts, and practice replacing them with thoughts that support you and your vision of your new life, you will be renewed. I am dedicating this work to your transformation. You are in the process of becoming empowered and filled with hope for the future. Soon you will celebrate conquering your fear and shame. Your bright and meaningful future awaits.

Remember, you are a powerful woman with a mighty heart, and you can create a fulfilling life on *your* terms. The pain of the past is a catalyst, propelling you into a life of choices and brilliant creations that can only be dimmed if you stop learning and moving forward. You are unstoppable!

I have practiced catching and replacing negative thoughts for many years. I can personally attest to the power of this method. I refer to it as "Catch Your Thoughts" (CYT). Because of the results I've experienced in my life, I firmly believe that our thoughts create our reality. I also believe that if we are thinking high-vibrational positive thoughts, the universe matches our high frequency. If, however, we are allowing ourselves to marinate in thoughts of fear and doubt, then our low vibrational thoughts will attract more of the same.

MY CLIENT, TINA, saw incredible results soon after she created her vision and life design, and then began focusing her thoughts on manifesting her desires. Tina created a PowerPoint slideshow of her new life. She needed a place of her own where she would feel safe and nurtured. She really wanted to be part of a supportive community. She also really wanted to have a sweet dog as a companion. Tina envisioned her new life with her dog by her side, living close to nature.

Each morning, Tina watched her PowerPoint slideshow, and really saw herself living that life. She allowed herself to feel the emotions she imagined she would feel, once she was living her ideal life. Whenever thoughts of disbelief crept in, such as the old negative loop of, "This is ridiculous. Nothing ever works out for me," she put up a stop sign in her mind and countered the defeating thoughts with the affirmation, "I am creating the life of my dreams."

Just three months later, Tina was attending a community event, when she ran into an old friend. Tina told Sherry about her recent divorce and her plans for a renewed life. Sherry mentioned that her sister lived in a tight-knit retirement community, where most of the women were single and enjoyed many activities together. Sherry said her sister was getting ready to put her house on the market, so she could move closer to her grandchildren. The park was situated near a small lake with a wooded nature trail and a fenced-in dog park.

Tina was able to make an offer on the house before it went on the market. Shortly thereafter, Tina adopted a very sweet golden Cocker Spaniel she named Hope. Tina has now added new slides to her PowerPoint. She is planning to purchase a small travel trailer, so she can begin traveling in camping caravans with solo women travelers.

This is the time to apply what you've learned, to attract the life you envision for yourself.

There is a large body of research about how our thoughts create our reality. If you're interested, you can search Google for more information on the placebo effect, mind over matter, manifestation and quantum physics. There are a multitude of YouTube videos to watch, as well. Citing research is beyond the scope of this book, but I'd like to share the names of some of my favorite authors who have written extensively on the subject. They are Dr. Wayne Dyer, Dr. Joe Dispenza, Dan Millman, Louise Hay, Michael Beckwith, Mike Dooley, Dawson Church, Shakti Gawain, Deepak Chopra, Oprah Winfrey and Lisa Nichols. I'm sure you've heard of the movie, *The Secret*. Dr. Wayne Dyer also made a very inspirational movie called, *The Shift*.

When you begin working to change your negative thoughts to positive ones reflecting the life you desire, it's important to pay attention to your emotions. If you suddenly begin to feel sad, anxious, or irritated, try to determine what you were thinking just before you began feeling that way. The sudden onset of these negative emotions is a clue that you were likely thinking about something negative. Once you identify what the thought was, counter it with a positive affirmation.

For example, when I was working as a counselor, sometimes I would suddenly begin feeling very stressed and anxious. I was able to trace this feeling to thinking, "There's too much to do, and I can never do everything that needs to be done." I worked on catching this thought every time I noticed these feelings creeping back in. I would put up a stop sign in my mind, and then replace it with the affirmation, "I'm making an important difference with the things I'm doing".

When you are successfully able to catch a negative loop in your mind, and replace it with a more positive thought, you are creating new neural pathways in your brain. As you become consistent at replacing those thoughts, your brain learns the new way of thinking, and it will become more natural to maintain a positive focus. Please go to my website to download a free thought-stopping worksheet.

When you are learning to replace your negative thoughts with positive ones, keep it light and make it into a game. Don't make it another item on your to-do list, because you may become overwhelmed and stop making progress. Remember to give yourself grace in this process. Don't focus on it obsessively. Allow your thoughts to come and go, and when you notice any negative feelings or repetitive destructive thoughts occurring, put up the mental stop sign, and replace it with a positive statement

What do you focus on? Your thoughts have power. You will manifest the things you focus on. For some people, thinking negatively about themselves and their life has become a habit. Self-defeating thoughts come and go on autopilot. If this describes you, it will take a concerted effort to create a new pattern for yourself. It may be helpful to keep a running journal of your recurring thoughts. Try to notice the major thoughts that are putting obstacles in your way and are most ingrained. Write them down in your journal and create a counter thought for each one.

When you recognize these thoughts popping up, you will then be able to stop yourself, and begin creating more supportive patterns in your brain. For example, if you find that you are thinking something several times a day, such as, "My life is such a mess," create a positive thought based on the progress you're making. Counter that thought with something like, "I am rebuilding a new and meaningful life for myself."

I believe it's important to choose counter statements that you feel are true. If you choose to tell yourself something that sounds good, but isn't realistic and doesn't resonate with you, you're setting yourself up for failure. Subconsciously, you are likely to tell yourself that the negative thought you always have is more realistic than the counter thought.

When you identify the major thoughts that are holding you back, memorize and practice the positive counter thoughts. It might be helpful to write them down and post them in a prominent place. This will provide a constant reminder that you are teaching your brain to catch self-defeating thoughts, and replace them with self-supporting thoughts.

Here are steps to follow to catch your thoughts:

1. Whenever you suddenly find yourself feeling a negative emotion, stop, breathe, and try to determine what you were just thinking.

2. When you identify the self-sabotaging thought, imagine a big red stop sign in your mind. Mentally envision that stop sign popping up and blocking the negative thought. For example, if you find yourself saying something defeating such as, "I never get things right!" envision the stop sign in your mind to break the thought pattern.

3. Replace the destructive thought with a true and self-supporting statement. For example, "That's not true. Today I handled that difficult client really well, and I helped my boss solve a problem this morning." Or, "I make mistakes like anyone, but I do many things right."

4. Write down the negative recurring thought and the positive counter thought. In this example, you would write down the negative statement, "I never get things right," and to the right of it, your positive statement, "I make mistakes like anyone, but I do many things right."

5. As you continue to identify recurring self-sabotaging thoughts, write them down and then write a positive counter thought. Fill out the sheet from my website or create your own and keep it where you can refer to it often. Remember that you are creating new neural pathways.

I KNOW SOMEONE—I'll call Nina—who has some of the worst luck I've ever seen. She told me that she doesn't like to be disappointed, so she expects the worst. Unfortunately, the worst is what she gets. When Nina had her kitchen remodeled, she worried that the contractor would make mistakes. She was dreading the completion of the work, because she thought that her new kitchen would be a disaster. Well, instead of having gorgeous new granite countertops, she found rough spots on the surface and she even found some cracks. Her cupboards were not plumb and the lines in her tile floors were uneven. It took two additional months for the contractor to get everything done correctly. Meanwhile, Nina could not use her kitchen and she was so upset she made herself sick. Her kitchen was a disaster, just as she expected. This is a tragic, and unnecessary, example of how you get what you expect.

In contrast, a friend of mine, I'll call Brenda, has a very positive outlook on life. Whenever something is happening that could go well or not so well, Brenda says, "Oh, it'll work out just fine." Brenda was going through a difficult time financially, when her only car began spewing antifreeze. She was close to an auto repair shop when it happened. The mechanic was able to quickly identify a tiny hose that had a crack in it. Brenda went next door to the auto parts store, squeaking in just 10 minutes before they were about to close, and they ordered the part for her. A friend drove by and saw her car there, so she stopped and gave Brenda a ride home. The next day the part came in, and the mechanic fixed Brenda's car for very little money.

I HAD A scary, yet surprisingly serendipitous, crisis in my motorhome. I was driving alone at night on a dark highway when I thought I drove over a tree branch. Suddenly I heard a horrible screeching sound, and saw sparks flying out the back. I had run over a piece of tire, and the tire had wrapped around my exhaust pipe, crushing it, and blowing out one of the tires.

I was completely shaken and scared about being stranded on a dark highway. A man pulled up in his car and whispered, "I'll help you." I just knew in my gut that the man was safe and that everything would be okay. It turned out that he had vocal cord damage, so he could only whisper. He helped me call a tow truck and directed traffic away from my RV. I now refer to that man as my "Whispering Angel." When I went to get the tire repaired, the technician told me that my tires were beginning to shred. If I hadn't hit that tire in the road, I most likely would have rolled my motorhome while traveling down the freeway. I believe I was protected and I'm very grateful.

THINKING POSITIVELY DOES not mean that you will not have challenges in life, but your thoughts do determine how things ultimately end up. They powerfully affect the way you feel as you go through each challenge. Do your own research and experiment with events that come up in your life. Try replacing your negative thoughts with positive ones and see what results you get. I believe you will find that transformation comes through replacing your self-defeating thoughts with ones that support the new life you are creating.

There is a popular quote by Lao Tzu that really sums up the power of your thoughts, and how they contribute to everything that happens in your life.

Watch your thoughts,
They become words.
Watch your words,
They become actions.
Watch your actions,
They become habits.
Watch your habits,
They become your character.

Watch your character,
It becomes your destiny.

Getting your thoughts in check will really transform your life more powerfully than anything else. Your emotions follow your thoughts, so you will be able to get off the rollercoaster of disturbing and paralyzing emotions. You will, of course, still experience sadness, anger, worry, and other strong emotions, but you will now know that you can most likely trace those feelings back to the thoughts that preceded them. You are the master of your destiny, and your destiny begins with your thoughts and the things you choose to focus on.

When you apply this principle and catch your thoughts, you will feel more in control of your life. In the next chapter, you will learn to turn your thoughts toward living in gratitude. Let's continue walking this journey together. You are transforming your life!

CHAPTER 7

STEP 5: DAILY GRATITUDE WILL CHANGE YOUR LIFE

The miracle of gratitude is that it shifts your perception to such an extent that it changes the world you see.

—DR. ROBERT HOLDEN

Y OU ARE ON a journey of discovery. You now have a strong foundation to build upon. You have a self-care toolbox, your values-based vision, a new life design, and you are gaining control of your thoughts to bring it all to fruition. Along this journey, you will encounter setbacks and challenges. This is when practicing gratitude is most important. There are times when you will be tempted to "catastrophize." In other words, it will feel like everything is falling apart, and all the progress you have made was for naught. You will have days when it seems that you have taken three steps forward and two steps back. You will feel that you have accomplished very little after working so very hard.

One technique that will help you to continue moving forward with creating your life of meaning and joy, is to practice feeling gratitude. Gratitude is wonderfully helpful when your life is moving along smoothly, but it's when you encounter bumps in the road, that it becomes *crucial*. Having control of your thoughts enables you to feel grateful much more quickly. Gratitude keeps your brain in a positive loop rather than spiraling down a dark hole of despair.

My client, Jenny, shared a powerful story with me. She created her vision and life design. She chose the value of "Vitality," because she was overweight and exhausted most of the time. She had begun a daily routine of walking in the nearby park for 30 minutes. She was beginning to feel more energetic, and had been feeling accomplished, when she tripped and sprained her ankle.

At first, her immediate thought was, "Of course, I always screw things up just when I start going in the right direction!" After she limped home and put ice on her ankle, Jenny continued to think negative thoughts. She was telling herself that she'd never be able to lose weight, and then she started thinking of how much she hated her body, and from there she spiraled into thinking about looking awful in her clothes and being unlovable. Jenny sat in her chair with swirling thoughts that were taking her to a very dark place. She noticed that her chest felt tight and her stomach was in knots. She felt like crying and considered giving up.

Then she instinctively took several deep breaths and sat with her feelings. She began to recognize them and peel them away one-by-one. She remembered the strategy of noticing the thoughts that created the bad feelings. She realized how her thoughts had quickly spiraled into negativity. She grabbed her journal from the table and looked for the exercise in which she'd identified those recurring thoughts and had written down positive counter thoughts. Jenny began to read them out loud. She then began to state out loud that she actually had made good progress. She had lost a few pounds. Her depression had lifted some by walking and being in nature each day. She had kept her commitment to herself to maintain a walking routine, and she was teaching herself to focus on positive, rather than negative, thoughts.

Jenny then moved into gratitude. She began naming things she was grateful for. She was grateful for her ability to walk. She was grateful to live near a park. She was grateful for her walking companion, her dog, Sadie. She was grateful to have the time to walk each day, and she was grateful to have a comfortable house to come home to. After Jenny listed 10 things she was grateful for, she noticed that her mood had lifted, and her ankle had even stopped throbbing. She was so excited to share with me that this process had helped to lift her out of the dark place she had sunken into, and how she had felt a sense of empowerment for the first time in a very long time.

Thinking of Jenny's story, let's review the steps she went through to turn the situation around:

IST

> She recognized that she was experiencing some very strong and negative emotions.

2ND

> Jenny sat with her feelings and took several deep breaths.

3RD

> She began to identify the thoughts that had preceded those emotions.

4TH

> She then picked up her journal where she had written down her self-defeating recurring thoughts and read the replacement counter thoughts she had created.

5TH

> Jenny began saying the positive thoughts out loud, countering the ones that had begun to send her spiraling downward.

6TH

> She then moved into gratitude. She began naming the many things in her life that she was grateful for.

7TH

> Following these steps and ending with gratitude lift-
> ed Jenny's mood and helped her to gain a clear and
> new perspective on her situation.

GRATITUDE SHIFTS YOUR perspective. When you are
thinking about how bad things are, and how things
never work out for you, things seem hopeless and bleak.
One thought leads to another, providing proof along
the way that causes you to think *even more* self-defeating
thoughts. You begin to see yourself as a victim of circum-
stance, instead of someone capable of creating the life
you desire.

When you choose gratitude, the world looks brighter.
You see possibilities, instead of roadblocks. Your brain
operates at a higher frequency, which in turn helps you
to see the signs ahead that point you in the direction you
need to go. Oprah Winfrey said, "What you focus on
expands, and when you focus on the goodness in your
life, you create more of it." I have found this to be very
true in my life.

When I got divorced in 1995, and I applied to graduate school, I had to take out loans to pay for all of it. I
was barely scraping by, but I knew I was creating better
opportunities for myself. I chose to focus on the fact that
my son and I were free from the tyranny of verbal abuse
and betrayal, rather than on the fact that I was broke,
alone, and raising a son without any help. I focused on

being in the moment and enjoying what I had. I looked forward to a brighter future.

As you continue your healing journey, gratitude is one of the most powerful tools you can carry in your toolbox. When you encounter setbacks, you can always pull it out to remember to be thankful for the things you do have, and to focus on what's going right.

You may be in a place right now where things are very challenging. It may seem that you are drowning in despair. That is a difficult place to be. But take a moment to think about what is going right for you. What can you be grateful for? Stop right now and list at least 10 things you are grateful for.

When you make the conscious choice to be grateful every day, you will begin to see your life transform. It's the same process you use for replacing negative thoughts.

1. Stop yourself when you feel sad, angry, or anxious.
2. Breathe and allow the emotions to move through you.
3. Identify the thoughts that led to the feelings.
4. Choose to find positive things to focus on. Reach for thoughts that will help you to feel the way you'd like to feel.

You do not have to be tossed like waves by your feelings. You are not at their mercy. You are in control, and you can choose to be empowered and to feel good.

When you are having difficulty staying in gratitude, return to your self-care toolbox. Sometimes your perspective on the world will become gray and murky. You may attempt to climb out of the darkness but find yourself sliding back into the hole. If you find that you're unable to pull yourself out of thinking dark thoughts, you very likely need rest and rejuvenation. Recovering from divorce and the major life changes and grief take a toll on your wellbeing. Remember to always return to self-care to allow yourself the time you need to heal and grow stronger.

Another way to fall into a pit is to engage in comparisons. When you begin comparing yourself to others, it's a sure way to become miserable. If you compare yourself to how you used to be, with the thought that you are now somehow less, you will begin drowning in unnecessary sadness. You are in control of your thoughts, and you have the power to change the way you think and feel.

If you are a person who really struggles with practicing gratitude, it can be helpful to have a gratitude partner. Find a friend or family member who will join with you in this powerful practice. Talk with them or text or email every day about the things you're grateful for, without lapsing into negativity. This simple accountability strategy will help your brain to begin looking for the evidence you need to share with your partner. You will find your thoughts turning toward the positive things to report.

What are the good things in your life you can choose to focus on? Even with a tragedy such as divorce, you now have any choice you desire. You are at the wheel. You are free. You are moving right along in learning and applying the first five of the eight steps that will transform your life.

1. Continue with your self-care schedule.
2. Keep making your decisions with your primary value in mind.
3. Remind yourself of your vision and life design and focus on them every day.
4. Keep catching self-defeating thoughts and replacing them with countering thoughts.
5. Stay in gratitude.

I commend you for making so much progress and for keeping your commitment to yourself. I trust that your heart is healing and your joy is increasing. You are truly a courageous woman!

In the next chapter, you will practice tapping into your internal guidance system. It's very exciting when you begin to see a connection between what you want and need, and then begin to find synchronicities that guide you in the direction of your dreams. Let's continue to build your skills and open the doors of your heart.

CHAPTER 8

STEP 6: RECEIVE GUIDANCE FROM YOUR INTERNAL GPS SYSTEM

You must strive to become much less susceptible to influences outside of yourself, and much more inclined to trust the instincts and feelings that lie within you.

—BOB PROCTOR

AT THIS POINT, you are practicing self-care. You have identified your values and have created a vision of the life you want to create. You are catching your negative thoughts and countering them with positive self-supporting ones. You are learning to live through the lens of gratitude. You have done a great deal of powerful work to prepare for your journey. I want to congratulate you on coming this far. You are learning to put yourself first, so you can heal and begin building a new life that is rooted in your personal truth and the wonder of the powerful woman you are. You are on your way!

When you tap into your higher self, on a daily basis, you will make profound progress in the direction that is truly best for you. Learning to listen to your own inner wisdom is a game-changer. I believe in God and divine intervention. In my life, I have felt guided and supported in incredible ways that have enabled me to trust in positive outcomes, even in very dark times. At this point in our lives, we have acquired great knowledge and life experience. We have a deep well of inner knowing to tap into. You can call it faith, or the Holy Spirit, or your higher self, or spirit. Dr. Wayne Dyer referred to it as "Source." To me, it's all the same, because I have no doubt whatsoever that we are guided and supported. I have a strong belief that life supports us. I do not believe that life conspires against us.

We use our intuition every day, often without realizing that we are engaging in something "mystical." You may start thinking about someone you haven't talked to in a while, and then they call you. Or you are somehow led down a street you don't usually go down, only to find the perfect parking spot. Or you hear a song on the radio that provides answers to a question you've been pondering. Things like this happen all the time, but we either don't tune in to the fact that we are being guided, or we ignore the "magic" and take it for granted.

When you begin focusing on tapping into your intuition and sixth sense on a regular basis, amazing things occur. I tell my clients to ask for direction from their higher source when they are grappling with a difficult problem. When you ask, you also need to stay tuned in to your intuition, so you can notice the signs and receive what you're looking for. This is where conscious practice is needed.

When I first started really wanting to tune in to receive guidance, I read the book, *Divine Intuition*, by Lynn Anderson. I started doing some of the exercises in her book and began strengthening my "intuition muscle." There are many ways to incorporate practice into your daily life. Begin testing yourself with fun little exercises. When you arrive to work, ask yourself something like, "When I go in the door, the first person I see will be wearing what color?" Notice what pops into your head. You might see a color, hear a tiny voice saying the color, or just sense a color. It's easy to feel silly and doubt yourself. That's exactly why it's important to play with this and practice. Make it a fun game. The more you practice and use this innate skill, the more you will learn to trust the guidance that is there for you.

I taught myself to see "yes" and "no" in my head. I'm not 100% accurate yet, but it gives me a way to quickly check with myself to see if something is good for me, or if I should take action. In my mind's eye, "yes" is up and "no" is down. The "yes" lights up for me. I might ask myself while shopping for vitamins, "Is this brand good for me?" and I will get an answer. The accuracy increases the more I use it. I've found it's helpful to make several comparisons, so I will test at least four different brands before choosing the one that had the brightest "yes."

One of the times I remember feeling really loved and protected by my inner guidance was in December of 2007. I got in my Toyota Camry to prepare to drive to work on a cold, icy morning. As I sat down I heard in my head, "Move the seat back!" It wasn't an audible voice, but it was different and more emphatic than my own thoughts. I tend to drive with my seat pretty far forward because my legs are short. I decided to heed the warning and immediately moved my seat back. Just 10 minutes later, as I approached an intersection on the highway, a lady driving a Suburban turned right in front of me. The airbags deployed and my car was totaled. I was bruised a little, but otherwise I was okay. I am certain that moving the seat back kept me from being injured by the airbag.

MY CLIENT, PAM, was walking down the sidewalk with her grandson behind her in his favorite little pedal car. He was singing happily as he pedaled behind her. She was enjoying the spring flowers and listening to the birds sing, when she heard a voice in her head say, "Stop, turn around!" She had been practicing increasing her intuitive skills, so she immediately responded to the voice. She turned around just in time to see her grandson pedaling his car toward the street, in the path of a car that was backing out of a driveway. She was able to stop her grandson just in time!

PAUSE FOR A moment to recall times when you've been guided. I bet you can come up with several examples within just a few minutes. Now identify how you received that guidance. Was it a voice in your head? Did you "see" a message? Did you sense it? Where did you feel it in your body? Was it in your mind? Did you feel it in your gut? Was it centered around your heart? Did it have a color or texture?

Skills in this area do vary somewhat, depending on the individual. I have a friend who sees and feels colors. Each color has its own temperature and texture for her. I know someone else who sees pictures in her mind. When she is thinking about a decision she has to make, she sees herself making the choice that is best for her. I see numbers in my head, and I hear song lyrics that are relevant to what I'm trying to figure out.

MY FRIEND JACKIE was in the midst of a nasty divorce. She and her partner were battling over the house they'd bought and renovated. She was in absolute turmoil because she had invested so much of her personal creativity and artistic flair into that house. She wanted to keep it, but her former partner was insisting on selling it. One day she was out walking along a nearby lake, agonizing over her dilemma. She took some deep breaths and pleaded for help. She asked, "Please show me what to do about the house." As soon as she asked, she heard the words, "Let it go," in her mind. Then she saw herself in a different house that felt very comforting and sacred.

As Jackie considered this guidance, she felt a release in her body. She felt the tension subside and she felt a warmth and inner peace. She stopped and looked out at the lake, and just to double check, asked the question, "Should I let go of the house?" She saw a "yes" in her mind. Jackie was able to let go of the struggle and let the house go. Eight months later, she found a house within walking distance of that very lake. She decorated it with her artwork and created a beautiful garden, where she incorporated her stonework, mosaic tiles, and an area she calls her "magical spot." The touches she has been able to add to her new place reflect her values and her vision for her new life.

What questions do you have to ask of your inner guidance? How do you receive information? Will you act on what you receive? It can be very helpful to start a dedicated "Intuition Journal." Write out your questions. Record answers that you receive, including how you receive them and what they feel like.

Just as with the other skills you're building, it is helpful to have a partner in this endeavor. If you don't know anyone who would like to practice increasing intuitive skills, go to the Facebook page and share your questions and the guidance you receive with the community. You might also decide to start a book club or a Meetup group, so you can practice the skills and share your progress with a group of women who are going through the same transition as you.

You possess great wisdom. Learn to tap into that wisdom, and you will add adventure and excitement to your life, as you receive direction and make progress. In the next chapter, you will be able to use the skills you have acquired up to this point to begin setting boundaries with others, by speaking your truth. You are now moving into becoming the empowered woman you're meant to be. My heart goes with you as you embark on this journey of healing and renewal.

CHAPTER 9

STEP 7: SPEAK YOUR TRUTH

*There is no greater agony than bearing an
untold story inside of you.*

—MAYA ANGELOU

HAVE YOU SPENT a great deal of your life taking care of others? Have you sacrificed yourself and your own needs and desires in the process? So many of us women have spent our lives taking care of spouses, children, and others, leaving our own needs unattended. It can become a habitual way of life to not even stop to consider what we might need. Now that you're over 50 and divorced, you can *really* do anything you desire. Your world may have crashed down around you, but it has also opened in unexpected ways. If you've always made accommodations for others, it's time for you to accommodate *yourself*. When you learn to speak your truth and stand up for the choices you want to make in your new life, you'll discover a feeling of freedom and empowerment. This can be difficult at first, because you might feel like you're being selfish. It's time to speak up for yourself and the dreams you hold. Don't allow your voice to be stifled any longer. You can be honest with yourself, and you can tell others what you think, *and* you can ask for what you need. Women often receive a great deal of pressure and push-back when they begin standing up for themselves. If this happens to you, remember that you will become depleted and unable to care for others, if you don't first care for yourself. Sacrificing yourself doesn't help anyone. In fact, I've learned that when you release the need to take care of others, those people learn and grow more than they would have if you continued to enable them.

There is a great classic book on this subject that I recommend you read, if you haven't already. It's *Codependent No More,* by Melody Beattie. So many of us have been conditioned to put everyone else first, to the detriment of our own physical and emotional well-being. If someone tries to shame you into returning to your old accommodating, self-sacrificing persona, breathe, stand your ground, and say something like, " I'm taking care of myself and creating balance in my life." Don't engage in getting defensive or explaining and justifying yourself. Go to the Facebook page or to someone you trust and receive encouragement and support to continue your journey of self-care and developing inner strength.

ROXANNE CAME TO me feeling depressed and depleted. She wasn't sure why she felt this way. She just knew that she couldn't continue living every day feeling half alive. As she talked, Roxanne described her family. She had three grown children and six grandchildren. Her youngest daughter, Lindsey, was a mother of two, and was constantly in and out of relationships and jobs. Lindsey often dropped the kids off for Roxanne to babysit, without even asking. Sometimes she would leave them for the entire day. Roxanne loved being a mother and grandmother, but she was exhausted and was no longer enjoying it.

In addition to taking care of the grandkids, Roxanne was a daily confidante for her son, Gary, who was struggling in his marriage and career. Roxanne listened patiently and tried to encourage him and give him ideas to solve his problems, but the daily negative conversations were draining her.

Roxanne belonged to the local community church. She loved the singing and fellowship each Sunday. It gave her solace and it was one of the only times during the week that she did something for herself. The assistant pastor had asked Roxanne to facilitate the Sunday school committee, and she had felt obliged to accept the role. Now she was spending an extra two or three hours at church every week. Roxanne thought she would enjoy having an activity of her own, but she ended up feeling more drained than ever.

As I spent time with Roxanne, I asked her if she had personal boundaries. She looked at me perplexed. She told me she wasn't sure what that meant. We worked together to identify Roxanne's values. I helped Roxanne think about some activities she would like to do if she didn't have so many outside demands on her time. Roxanne smiled as she talked about how she enjoyed making stained glass and pottery. She had stopped, because she had used her spare bedroom to set up a playroom for the grandkids.

Roxanne readily admitted that Lindsey was taking advantage of her generosity with babysitting the grandkids. She had tried to come up with a way to tell her that she couldn't keep dropping off the kids unannounced, but Roxanne was afraid of losing her daughter and the bond she had with the kids.

Roxanne's life was clearly out of balance because she wasn't speaking her truth. She was growing resentful of her daughter, and she didn't want to have negative feelings toward her. She desperately needed time for herself that she wasn't getting. Roxanne needed to find the words to tell Lindsey that she couldn't watch the kids four or five days every week. She decided to set boundaries with her daughter, so she could free up some of her time to do things that would energize her.

Roxanne and I worked together to come up with a diplomatic but emphatic statement, sandwiched between positive and kind words. This is what Roxanne said to Lindsey: "Lindsey, I love you so much, and I'm proud of you for looking for work to support your family. I love seeing the grandkids, but I am feeling completely exhausted. I need to set up a schedule with you, so I can balance having time to rest and do things I enjoy, while also offering you occasional support."

Lindsey responded well overall. She understood that her mom was tired and needed a break. They set up a schedule for three hours of babysitting twice a week. After one week of following the schedule, Lindsey brought the kids a third time, unannounced. Roxanne held her boundary and told her she would not be able to watch the kids, because she had other plans. Lindsey was frustrated, but she obliged her mom and left.

Roxanne gained confidence after her success with Lindsey. She then resigned from the church committee, because she wanted to feel joyful about going to church again.

She also set boundaries with her son, Gary. She told Gary that she loved talking to him, but she wanted to hear more about good things that were happening in his life. She asked Gary to choose one day each week on which he would talk about his problems with his marriage and his career. On the other days, Roxanne told him, she could no longer hear about his struggles, because she worried about him, and it was wearing on her. Gary agreed, and Roxanne was able to enjoy their calls much more. In fact, Gary's mood improved because he was actively looking for positive things to share with his mom.

Roxanne decided that having the space to work on making stained glass was very important to her mental and emotional well-being. She cleared out the spare bedroom for herself, and used a cozy corner of her living room to set up a tent as a play area for her grandkids. She purchased the supplies she needed to get back to making stained glass and set up her work area in the bedroom. She worked on her beautiful creations twice a week and enjoyed every minute of it. She began feeling energized and excited to get going each day. She even found herself having more joy and energy for her grandkids.

THIS STORY OF Roxanne is a beautiful illustration of how speaking your truth and living authentically can improve your life greatly. Becoming truly authentic is a process that takes time, but the steps you've taken so far in this book have given you the tools you need. You must learn to tune in to your inner knowing and become aware of the demands and restrictions others place on you, as well as those you've imposed on yourself. When you are clear on what you value and believe, you develop clarity for setting boundaries and seeking that which you truly desire.

When you live to please and accommodate others, and forget about yourself, you become depleted. You are ignoring your center and your truth. You end up feeling spent and resentful.

Speaking your truth does *not* mean that you say every thought that comes into your mind. It comes from a place of strength and belief in yourself and your value as an individual. Sometimes people swing the pendulum from stifling their voice, to the opposite extreme of being brash and having no filters in expressing their newly empowered voice.

CARY RENTED A space in the community where I lived when I first moved out. She had a disagreement with her neighbor over a scuffle between their dogs, right after she moved in. Before she even got acquainted with anyone in the neighborhood, she began openly criticizing her neighbor to anyone who would listen. She loudly proclaimed her dislike of the man and cried angrily about the injustice of her situation. She even had a discussion on her phone with an attorney, in a common area where others could hear. She was immediately shunned. Almost everyone in the community avoided her.

AT FIRST GLANCE it might seem that Cary was speaking her truth because she wasn't stifling her feelings of anger and injustice. But Cary was out of balance. She didn't take the time to get to know anyone on a personal basis. She blasted her new neighbors with her negative emotions. She didn't listen to anyone to build trust. She didn't take the time to build a relationship and validate anyone else's thoughts or feelings, but she expected them to do this for her. It was one-sided and extreme, and she found herself alone and ignored. If you approach "speaking your truth" as if you have a license to blast people, you will push people away. You will miss out on the rewards of open-hearted communication.

Speaking your truth can be done diplomatically, from the heart, in a way that does not burn bridges with others. Some people will become defensive, but if you are centered and speak from the heart, asking for what you need, that is all you can do. You have no control over how people choose to react. More often than not, people will respect the fact that you are being authentic.

You have a right to your feelings. We often try to explain away the surrounding circumstances and end up denying or stuffing our feelings. It's important to express yourself and to address situations that are upsetting and hurtful. Speaking your truth leads to peace of mind.

Denying yourself, in time, leads to despair and resentment. When you are not able to speak your truth, your body, mind, and spirit suffer. You feel stifled, and it's difficult to move into being the very best version of yourself.

If you are a person who has always said "yes," and you have gone out of your way to accommodate and please everyone, be aware that people will want you to return to your former behavior. Without even realizing it, they will test you and possibly even chastise you, because the change is also uncomfortable for them. They had previously been able to count on you behaving in a predictable way. It's important, and acceptable, for you to stand your ground. Remember, when you speak your truth, you are also modeling the most effective and empowering behavior for others.

Being authentic is liberating and empowering, and your relationships will be stronger and healthier as a result. Once you've begun to behave and speak with authenticity, you will feel uneasy when you are not speaking your truth.

If you are someone who has never had the opportunity to feel safe speaking your truth, due to abusive relationships, I highly recommend you receive therapy for at least a few months. It's important to receive support and guidance while you learn to speak your truth. You will need direction and encouragement in applying these skills while you strip away the fears you have become accustomed to living with.

I have done a great deal of work in this area and continue to build my skills in speaking my truth in a variety of situations. I grew up with a dad who would get very angry if we became upset or emotional. If I cried more than just a few tears, I was criticized and called "crazy." I was expected to be quiet, and unemotional. Consequently, I learned to be a master peacemaker and accommodator.

At the end of this book, you will learn about the 5-week healing pilgrimage I took. That trip helped me more than I could ever express. I gained confidence by facing my fears. I managed every situation that came up on my trip. I made decisions for myself and I learned to trust my gut. The journey enabled me to develop a new identity and helped me to trust myself more than ever. As a result, I also improved at speaking my truth and standing up for myself. I will take women on healing journeys, and I hope you can join us on one of our life-changing adventures.

Women receive many mixed messages from society. There is a great deal of pressure to be quiet and to not question the status quo. Fortunately, the pendulum is swinging, and women are gradually learning the value of speaking up and asserting themselves. We still have a long way to go, but our collective wisdom and power are definitely on the rise. The growth that you make and the example you set will help young girls and your family members who follow you, to grow up in a world that is more equal, just, and based in truth.

Here are some steps to take when you need to speak your truth:

1. When you become aware that your voice is being stifled, take some time before responding. Get away from the situation.

Breathe deeply several times, get centered and catch any thoughts that can be self-defeating. Give yourself the space to decide how best to respond.

2. Ask the person for a time to talk when you won't be interrupted.

3. Before beginning the conversation, drop into your heart, let go of fear, and locate your inner place of strength. When you're feeling grounded, begin the conversation with something positive, and express the outcome you'd like to see. For example, "I need to explain my thoughts and feelings."

4. Express your feelings and desires from a place of love, but also with firmness. Don't waver on your stance or downplay the validity of your position.

5. Focus on using the word "I" rather than "you." Explain yourself by stating, "When this occurred, I felt shut down. I'd like to explain my position".

6. Stay calm and stay centered as you wait for the person to respond.

7. Don't back down from your truth by saying anything like, "Oh, it's okay. I must be too sensitive." You have a right to your feelings and you have the right to speak your truth.

8. Stand your ground and continue to expect the person to respect your wishes. Leave the situation from a place of love and personal power.

CHAPTER 10
OVERCOME SETBACKS AND KEEP GOING!

I don't want to live a life of wondering what could have been...

I want to capture every moment and live it to my fullest potential!

—ANONYMOUS

THINGS WILL GO wrong. Obstacles will arise. People will try to convince you that you should just be safe and stay with the status quo. You will feel fear and you'll have times when you question whether you're moving in the right direction. But if you have carefully created your vision, and you are taking steps toward it, you will achieve your goals. Circumstances may arise that will prevent you from reaching specific outcomes you had in mind, but in my experience, even though it's discouraging and upsetting at the time, it most always leads you in a better direction.

It's so important, during these trying times, to keep your faith and to trust yourself. Keep going no matter what! Your plans might change along the way, but never give up on your dreams. You don't have to live a life of regret, wondering what could have been. You do not have to let fear envelop and paralyze you. You have a spark inside that longs to be ignited. Dr. Wayne Dyer used to say, "Don't die with your music still in you." You have a purpose and you have contributions to make that *only you* can make. You can have a joyful, purposeful life and you can leave this life knowing that you lived it fully, without regrets.

I HAD SPENT the entire summer of 2017 fixing up my house to be a vacation rental so I could travel and build my business while I was on the open road. That was my ultimate dream. My dream didn't turn out at all the way I thought it would.

My contractor had been doing minor work inside my home, and he had done a nice job. When it was time to replace the rotting deck, he told me he needed $6,000 to purchase the materials. I sold my van to pay for the work. He took the money and promptly got arrested for past offenses. His wife had the money in their car, and yet told me, "It got stolen." The money was gone! I was completely devastated! The rental season was coming to an end, and I couldn't even enter the house through my front door. After pouring time and money into fixing my house to be rented, I had been completely thwarted!

I decided to lick my wounds by taking a trip to the Olympic Peninsula in Washington state. I had stepped out on a limb and purchased a motorhome that spring.

I didn't know how to operate it, or how to maneuver it through traffic and tight spaces, but I didn't let that stop me. Since I had taken the 9,000-mile trip in my van, I could not get traveling out of my blood. I longed for the open road, so I bought a small, older Class C Itasca Navion. I struck out on the three-hour trip, gripping the steering wheel with white knuckles, as I drove through a construction zone. I desperately needed to get out of eastern Washington to escape the smoke from surrounding wildfires. It had been a long, hot, windy summer, and the latest fire was within eight miles of my house.

After spending one night in Port Townsend, I knew that was where I wanted to live. I had no idea how it would come about, but I knew in my gut that I had found my home where I would begin my new life. This was a very unexpected but exciting change in my plans.

That was in August. In September, I found a park to live in and ordered my 395-square-foot tiny home. In October, I moved my mom into a lovely assisted living apartment with a view of the water. I put my house on the market and began packing. After being on the market for about 10 days, I received the first offer. I was so excited that doors were opening wide for my new life. Until the offer fell through...

I took my motorhome to the new park, and that's when I ran over the tire on the highway. I left my damaged vehicle in Port Townsend and went back to my house, holding my breath, praying that it would sell. I started to get scared that things might not work out, because I had experienced several setbacks. I had to lower the price on the house. Winter wasn't far away, and I desperately wanted to move before the snow began piling up.

The park where I was staying in my motorhome was a few blocks from my mom's new place, but my space was right next to a gas station. I told God that I was grateful to have a space in such a lovely town, but I really wanted to be in nature, not next to a noisy, very brightly lit gas station.

I continued packing and downsizing by selling about 70% of my belongings. I reserved a moving truck because the snow was coming soon. I moved my belongings between snowstorms. That's when a solid offer came in on my house. Then, in November, I found the beautiful community I now live in, on the bay, with a huge area for the dogs to run, a nature trail, and amazing residents. Happily, it's far from the gas station.

Along the way, while rebuilding my life and pursuing my dreams, I have encountered many obstacles. I have cried a lot of tears. I have certainly had my share of dark days, but my vision is clear and I believe the universe is supporting me. I trusted that my dashed plans would surely lead to better ones. I have great determination and will not quit! I see every challenge as an opportunity to learn and grow. I view setbacks as guidance that I can go in a better direction. I trust my intuition and seek guidance constantly.

If I had given up when the contractor stole my money, I wouldn't have sold my house and discovered my dream place to live. I would still be stuck suffering through hot summers and digging out of snowy winters. I now live in a wonderfully supportive community that feeds my soul. I live near the water, which satisfies a deep longing I'd had for many years.

You will have setbacks, too, but if you lose your faith and confidence and give up, you will remain stuck and you'll miss out on experiencing transformational change. Don't allow your journey to come to an abrupt halt. Take the detour and keep going! Your circumstances will not change unless you make a commitment to yourself, and don't back down for anything.

You have created your vision, you identified your values, you designed the life you long to live, you are changing your thoughts, practicing gratitude, and tuning in to your intuition. You have traveled quite a distance already. When the journey does not unfold as expected, trust that it is unfolding in your favor. You are supported. It's all about perspective. You can choose to view dead end signs as restrictive and limiting, or you can view them as indicators that you need to turn around and find a new route, continuing the adventure.

You can always choose to be in turmoil, or to believe, stay in gratitude, and be happy. Happiness and joy flow from within. You will not find your joy or peace anywhere but within yourself. If I had known how many challenges I would face, and continue to face, I might not have made such major changes in my life. But I have no regrets. I love my life, and so will you, if that's what you decide to do.

When I first moved out on my own, I struggled with loneliness mostly in the evenings. It was a very difficult transition after being part of a couple for 21 years. I felt empty and sad. I wasn't sure how to fill my time. Sometimes I ate too much to fill the void. I felt lost for a while. I didn't allow myself to get stuck there, though.

I started doing research on traveling solo. I read a book called *Vanabode on $20 a Day*, and that led me to do more research on converting a van for camping. I watched YouTube videos, took notes, listened to podcasts, read other books, and began making plans to convert my Kia van into a camper van. I decided to visit my brother in Chicago. I found a new passion and kept at it. It turned out to be my saving grace. I ended up taking a 9,000-mile healing journey that you'll read about in the next chapter. It was life changing!

> *Tell me what it is you plan to do with your one wild and precious life.*
>
> —MARY OLIVER

Will you transform your pain into triumph? Will you use this window of opportunity to create the life of your dreams? Will you stop at nothing to pursue your passions? Are you prepared to do whatever it takes to achieve your goals and to become a woman of passion and purpose?

You can decide right now to become the best version of yourself. No one is stopping you but you. Go after your dreams with all you've got! You now have the tools you need to transform your life. Don't push the toolbox under your bed and forget about it. Take it out every day and use the tools you have acquired to build your new life.

Time passes. You can choose to wait for the perfect moment that will likely never come. You can plan and ponder and put this book on the shelf and go back to being in limbo and feeling stuck. In six months or a year, you'll still be there. You'll still be miserable and confused. You can spend that same amount of time or less, though, getting in touch with the core of who you are and who you're meant to be. Choose life. Choose transformation and celebration. Live life to the fullest! If you want to make quicker progress, you can work with me on an individual basis, or you can apply to participate in my signature coaching program to become an "Unbreakable Woman with a Courageous Heart," and to use your transformative story to help lift others up. I look forward to reading your story on the private Facebook page. You are the author of your life. Make your story one of greatness! Together we can create your magnificent life!

After you have completed this book, I recommend that you continue learning by starting a Meetup group or book club based on the system you've just learned. It is true that those who teach learn the most. I also strongly suggest that you go back through the book periodically, to check your progress. Stay involved with your Facebook tribe. Record your progress and seek support when you encounter obstacles. Continue to build your skills. Share my book with friends and family, so you can support and celebrate each other's successes.

You are in the process of rewriting your story. Be the victorious one who leaves a powerful legacy. Do it for yourself, do it for other women, do it for young girls, and for those who will follow in your footsteps. You are a powerful woman with a mighty heart, and I believe in you. You've got this! Don't pull over and park on the shoulder when life puts up roadblocks. Keep your engine running and take the detour. You will find your way, I promise! Now you're ready to move on to step 8. You are in the final stretch! I commend you for sticking with this process toward creating a life you love.

CHAPTER 11

STEP 8: OVERCOME FEARS AND TAKE A HEALING JOURNEY

Women need real moments of solitude and self-reflection to balance out how much of ourselves we give away.

—Barbara De Angelis

I left my marriage in February of 2016. That June, after completing my 19TH year as a school counselor, I loaded up my converted van and my dog, Anni, and embarked on a grand adventure. I hadn't camped since I was about 12 years old. Some of my friends and family thought my plans were too risky. They were concerned that I might break down on the road or be vulnerable to "bad people" because I was a woman traveling alone in a van. I didn't spend time thinking about what could go wrong. I just felt strongly that it was something I needed to do. I took precautions; I bought AAA coverage, had bear spray, and planned where I wanted to go. Of course, I had the best protection of all, my German Shepherd mix dog who would become anyone's best friend immediately upon meeting them!

The plan was to take my time getting to Chicago, seeing sights along the way. Then around July 4TH, I would arrive to spend a week visiting my brother and his wife. After that, I knew I would strike out to somewhere in the Midwest, but I wasn't exactly sure where.

I was on the road for five weeks and traveled a total of 9,000 miles. I watched the sun set over the Badlands of South Dakota, visited an ancient Native American site in Minnesota, spent the day at the Lincoln Museum in Illinois, camped in Door County in Wisconsin with my brother, sat by a lake in Ohio as lightning bugs flashed around me, waited out a storm on Lake Erie as Anni and I hunkered down in a shaking van, walked along the waterfront in Pittsburgh, meandered along trails by the Finger Lakes in New York, stood and marveled at the immense power of Niagara Falls, walked into the infamous cornfield at the Field of Dreams in Iowa, and hiked under the big sky at Glacier National Park.

Of course, the places I saw and experiences I had were phenomenal. I met so many wonderful people along the way, but the benefits I personally reaped from the trip are still difficult to quantify. I think what was most valuable to me about this epic trip was that I faced my fears, and I was completely on my own with my thoughts and excitement about the adventure of it all. I gained a great deal of confidence in myself and my resourcefulness. I made my own decisions, followed my instincts, and learned to trust myself more than ever. I spent most of the trip alone and learned to love it!

I cannot emphasize enough how important it is to learn to enjoy being alone. You won't be alone forever, even though it may feel like that sometimes. Before you can become whole and truly give authentic love to others, you must learn to be comfortable in your own skin and love yourself. That trip helped me to do that.

Have you ever taken a trip by yourself? I now belong to some Facebook groups for solo women travelers and RV'ers. There are a lot of women who are enjoying the thrill of adventure and the joy of traveling alone. There are also groups of women who travel in camping caravans. If camping isn't your thing, there are still lots of ways to travel alone to build up your confidence and learn to trust your intuition. There is a great program I hope to try someday, called Road Scholar. In this program, you travel in groups to sites around the world, where you also learn about the world in a group of like-minded people.

If you're not quite ready for world travel, you can begin to get comfortable traveling alone by taking day trips to places you've never been before. Perhaps there are museums or parks in your hometown that you've never visited. Start by taking one day each week to explore some of these places, then you can begin branching out from there.

MY FRIEND, DONNA, hadn't even gone to a movie or out to dinner alone. It was very challenging for her at first. She felt nervous and self-conscious the first time she sat in a movie theater by herself. She was uncomfortable sitting in a restaurant without a companion to talk to. She didn't know what to do with herself. Eventually, she realized going out alone was a sort of rite of passage that she needed to experience. After the first time she took herself out to dinner, she felt exhilarated and empowered, because she had done the very thing she had been so afraid to do.

About two years after Donna overcame her fear of having a night out on her own, she booked a trip to Australia by herself. She stayed for two weeks and had the time of her life. She met new people, went on several exciting excursions, and didn't want to leave to return home!

WHAT IS SOMETHING you're afraid to do? What can you do to step outside your comfort zone?

My very first solo trip, before going across the country in my van, was a few hours away to Ashland, Oregon, with Anni. I rented a funky little cottage on HomeAway.com. The owners were artists and they had a beautiful garden filled with their sculptures and birdhouses. I wandered around downtown, drove into the hills, and hung out at Emigrant Lake. Then I drove from there to the Oregon Coast. I stayed in an oceanfront hotel and fell asleep to the sound of the waves crashing. I walked along the beach with Anni and picked up shells and driftwood for craft projects. I envision myself traveling with a special companion someday, but until then, I have learned to enjoy traveling alone.

Sometimes at first, when I travel alone, I struggle with feeling lost and unsure of how to spend my time. It can be difficult to make plans and get going in the morning, but I've learned to put some things in a small backpack and set out to explore. Before long I begin to have a wonderful time.

I believe so strongly in the power of taking risks and facing your fears, that I will be taking women on camping caravans and healing retreats. Would you like to come along? Doing something so special for yourself and stepping out on your own, as well as having the camaraderie of other women, will be life changing. I guarantee you'll return a different person, a more whole, confident, and resourceful woman with passion and purpose.

If you'd like to know more about healing journeys for women, visit my website:

www.MidlifeRenewalCoach.com

I would love you to join us for an epic and healing adventure!

I learned my strengths and my weaknesses. I experienced the exhilaration of the ups and the despairs of the lows and most of the feelings in between... I learned courage and I learned it myself.

— ANN STIRK

CONCLUSION

Life is no brief candle to me. It is a sort of splendid torch, which I have got a hold of for the moment, and I want to make it burn as brightly as possible before handing it on to future generations.

—GEORGE BERNARD SHAW

I COMMEND YOU for reading through this entire book. You invested in yourself. You made a commitment and kept it. I hope your heart has been stirred and your soul inspired. You have been given the gift of tools you can apply to rebuild your life. You have received encouragement and you've read stories of other women just like yourself. I'd like to reach out to you across space and time to give you a hug and to look into your eyes. I'd like to say to you, "You are amazing. You have a good heart and you are worthy of following your dreams. You have so much to give, and there is no one on this Earth who has the life experience, knowledge, and unique gifts that you possess. You matter, and you can rebuild your life to one of joy and purpose, and you can truly make a difference for others. This is your time to re-create yourself into the fullness of your being that has been suppressed for so long."

I wrote much of this book either sitting in my sunny bay window in my kitchen, or in my motorhome parked by the water. Each time I sat down to write and pour out my soul to you, I breathed deeply, dropped into my heart, and infused my message with love. This book is my love letter to the women who have been hurt, let down, betrayed, disappointed, shamed, and led to believe they are somehow unlovable and unworthy. You are beautiful! You have so much to give. When you release your fear, you will be filled with joy and hope. Fear is the opposite of love. Make the choice to live your life in love. Lead with your heart. Discover your message, and then share it, to inspire *others* to live their lives being all *they're* meant to be.

Now is the time for your new beginning. Anything you've ever longed for, wished you could do, fantasized that perhaps "one day" you could achieve, can now be yours. I know, that is a bold statement. I'll venture a guess that you read that and thought something like, "Me? I don't have the money, or the talent, or the skills. I'm too old. I'm past my prime. It's just too late for me." I assure you, it is never too late! Your life will not become grand overnight, but if you work through this book, seek support, learn to love yourself, feed your soul, face your fears, and refuse to give up, you will rebuild your life and you will be happy. You will live a life of meaning and purpose.

Will you resign yourself to the alternative? Will you stay stuck, miserable, and unfulfilled? It is up to you, but you certainly do not have to settle for a directionless and small life. I pour my heart into my work with women, because I truly believe women are powerful and amazing beyond words, and they deserve to live spectacular lives. We have been given false messages about our weaknesses, inadequacies, and imperfections. It's time to stand together in strength and celebration! We deserve happiness and fulfillment!

> *Wisdom means to choose now what will make sense later. I am learning every day to allow the space between where I am and where I want to be to inspire me and not terrify me.*
> —*Tracee Ellis Ross*

Move forward, in the direction of your dreams every day, even if it's in small increments. Surround yourself with people who support and inspire you. Keep the momentum going. Utilize the tools you've been given. Nurture yourself, on a daily basis. When you have decisions to make, breathe deeply, drop into your heart, and ask for guidance. Then follow your instincts and go forward. You are on a healing journey. You have life lessons to learn. You have great wisdom to draw from. You are in this life to contribute the unique gifts and talents you've developed. What will your legacy be? What great things will you accomplish?

Believe in yourself. I believe in you. You've got this!

ABOUT THE AUTHOR

NANCY OSIER RETIRED from counseling after 20 years, to pursue her dream of building her life coaching business, Midlife Renewal Coach. She spent her career counseling families and children with an emphasis on anger management, conflict resolution, communication skills, leadership, and crisis response and recovery.

She earned her Master's degree in Counseling Psychology from Central Washington University. Nancy was a foster parent for seven years and worked as a foster care case manager. Before returning to college at the age of 30, Nancy worked in the insurance business for 10 years. She became certified as a life coach through the Coach Training Academy in 2011 and was also trained in Stephen Covey's "7 Habits of Highly Successful People."

Nancy has a passion for helping women live empowered lives, full of purpose and passion. She left her counseling career in 2017 to pursue her dream. She started her life over completely at 54. She sold her house, bought a tiny home and a motorhome, moved from the desert to the Olympic Peninsula near the water, and moved her mother nearby to care for her.

She is an author, entrepreneur, and motivational speaker. Nancy is excited to bring her knowledge and life experience to the world with her coaching program, seminars, book, speaking engagements, healing retreats, and travel adventures for women who wish to rebuild their lives in a powerful way.

Nancy will be featured in *Oprah* magazine and *Entrepreneur* in the Pacific Northwest region in April of 2019. Discover more about what Nancy has to offer at www.MidlifeRenewalCoach.com and on her Facebook page, Life Coach Nancy Osier. You can also email Nancy at:

lifecoachnancyosier@gmail.com

or

divorcedafter50@yahoo.com

NANCY HAS A passion for helping women reinvent themselves to truly live life to the fullest.

If you'd like to go further and work directly with Nancy, she offers several coaching programs to meet everyone's needs:

- Weekly one-hour private coaching sessions for up to 12 weeks.
- Online Group-Coaching Webinars with a Community of like-minded women. This is a 6-week program that includes access to a private Facebook page, lessons that delve deeply into the 8 steps, weekly Q&A, and a private coaching session with Nancy.
- Nancy's Signature 8-week Group Coaching Program is called "Unbreakable Women with Courageous Hearts". This includes everything listed above, with the addition of a 3-day Live Event that will be held each quarter in different locations across the U.S.. Space for this intensive and life-changing program is limited, so email Nancy today if you're interested in attending to completely transform your life.

- Nancy also holds weekend renewal beach retreats on Whidbey Island in Washington state.

Nancy will soon have other books published. To stay informed, please follow her on Facebook at "Life Coach Nancy Osier", visit her website and sign up with your email at www.MidlifeRenewalCoach.com, or email her directly at lifecoachnancyosier@gmail.com

JOIN NANCY'S MOVEMENT OF EMPOWERED WOMEN LIVING LIVES OF PURPOSE AND JOY

51041599R00070

Made in the USA
Columbia, SC
15 February 2019